Another Cosmopolitanism

Seyla Benhabib

With Commentaries by
Jeremy Waldron
Bonnie Honig
Will Kymlicka

Edited and introduced by
Robert Post

D0068444

UNIVERSITY PRESS

2006

OXFORD

UNIVERSITY PRESS

Oxford University Press, Inc., publishes works that further
Oxford University's objective of excellence
in research, scholarship, and education.

Oxford New York
Auckland Cape Town Dar es Salaam Hong Kong Karachi
Kuala Lumpur Madrid Melbourne Mexico City Nairobi
New Delhi Shanghai Taipei Toronto

With offices in
Argentina Austria Brazil Chile Czech Republic France Greece
Guatemala Hungary Italy Japan Poland Portugal Singapore
South Korea Switzerland Thailand Turkey Ukraine Vietnam

Published by Oxford University Press, Inc.
198 Madison Avenue, New York, New York 10016

www.oup.com

Oxford is a registered trademark of Oxford University Press

Library of Congress Cataloging-in-Publication Data

Benhabib, Seyla.
Another cosmopolitanism/Seyla Benhabib; with commentaries
by Jeremy Waldron, Bonnie Honig, Will Kymlicka;
edited and introduced by Robert Post.
p.cm.—(Berkeley Tanner lectures)
Includes bibliographical references and index.

ISBN-13 978-0-19-536987-8

1. Cosmopolitanism. 2. Law—Philosophy. 3. Human rights.
4. Citizenship. 5. World citizenship. I. Waldron, Jeremy.
II. Honig, Bonnie. III. Kymlicka, Will. IV. Post, Robert.
V. Title. VI. Series.

JZ1308.B48 2006
306.01—dc22   2006040013

Printed in the United States of America
on acid-free paper

Acknowledgments

The following text is a much revised version of the Tanner Lectures, which I was asked to deliver at the University of California in Berkeley in March 2004. I thank the Berkeley University Tanner Committee and in particular Samuel Sheffler, Martin Jay, David Hollinger, and Aihwa Ong for their questions and comments, and Judith Butler and Wendy Brown for their hospitality during this occasion.

I am grateful to Bonnie Honig, William Kymlicka, and Jeremey Waldron, whose deep and engaging comments have taught me a great deal.

Robert Post has been an invaluable friend, critic, and interlocutor as this volume has taken shape and at many points has helped me sharpen my arguments.

Several other colleagues have commented on various aspects of these discussions: Tom McCarthy, Nancy Fraser, Rainer Bauboeck, and Jim Sleeper, my husband, have made important observations along the way.

Turkuler Isiksel has joined this project in its final phases and has provided invaluable editorial and bibliographic assistance. I thank her for the good work.

SEYLA BENHABIB
October 2005

Contents

REPLY TO COMMENTATORS

SEYLA BENHABIB

List of Contributors

SEYLA BENHABIB is Eugene Meyer Professor of Political Science and Philosophy at Yale University. She is internationally regarded for her research and teaching on nineteenth- and twentieth-century European social and political thought, particularly German idealism, Max Weber, the Frankfurt School, and Hannah Arendt. She is renowned for her contributions to the history of modern political theory and the foundations of ethics, and is also recognized as a notable feminist theorist.

Born in 1950 in Istanbul, Turkey, Benhabib received her B.A. in philosophy from Brandeis University in 1972 and her Ph.D. in philosophy from Yale University in 1977. Past academic and honorary positions include chairing the Committee on Degrees in Social Studies at Harvard University from 1997 to 2001, where she served as Professor of Government from 1993 to 2000 and was senior research fellow at the Center for European Studies. Since 2001, she has been director of Yale's Program in Ethics, Politics, and Economics.

A prolific writer, Benhabib has published numerous articles and books including *The Claims of Culture: Equality and Diversity in the Global Era* (2002); *Transformations of Citizenship: Dilemmas of the Nation-State in the Era of Globalization* (2000); and *Situating the Self: Gender, Community, and Post-Modernism in Contemporary Ethics* (1992), which was awarded the American Educational Studies Association's Critics' Choice Award in 1993. Benhabib's more recent publications include *The Reluctant Modernism of Hannah Arendt* (1996; new edition 2003) and *The Rights of Others: Aliens, Residents, and Citizens* (2004), which received the Ralph Bunche Award of the American Political Science Association and was selected best book in social philosophy (2004) by the North American Society for Social Philosophy. Benhabib has been a member of the American Academy of Arts and Sciences since 1995, and in January 2004 she received an honorary degree from the Humanistic University of Utrecht. She has previously delivered the Gauss Lectures at Princeton University (1999), the Spinoza Lectures at the University of Amsterdam (2000), and the Seeley Lectures at the University of Cambridge (2002). She is president of the Eastern Division of the American Philosophical Association in 2006.

Bonnie Honig is Professor of Political Science, Northwestern University, and Senior Research Fellow, American Bar Foundation, Chicago. She is a notable scholar in the areas of democratic and feminist theory. Her research focuses specifically on questions of legitimacy, constitutionalism, nationalism, cosmopolitanism, and the politics of immigration and law. She has written extensively on modern and contemporary political thinkers such as Kant, Rousseau, Nietzsche, John Rawls, Hannah Arendt, and Jacques Derrida and has published essays in *Political Theory, the American Political Science Review, Social Text, Social Research, Boston Review,* and elsewhere. From 1999 to 2002, she was Book Review Editor for *Political Theory.*

Honig is the author of *Democracy and the Foreigner* (2001), the subject of a 2002 American Political Science Association theme panel. Her first book, *Political Theory and the Displacement of Politics* (1993) was awarded the 1994 Scripps Prize for the Best First Book in Political Theory from the Foundations of Political Thought branch of the American Political Science Association. She is also editor of *Feminist Interpretations of Hannah Arendt* (1995), coeditor of *Skepticism, Individuality and Freedom: The Reluctant Liberalism of Richard Flathman* (2002), and coeditor of the *Oxford Handbook of Political Thought* (2006). Honig is currently writing a book titled *Future Perfect.*

Honig received her B.A. in political science from Concordia University, Montreal, in 1980. She received her M.Sc. from the London School of Economics in 1981 and her M.A. in 1986 and Ph.D. in 1989 in political theory from the Johns Hopkins University. Honig taught at Harvard from 1989 to 1997 and has been a fellow at the Center for Advanced Studies in the Behavioral Sciences at Stanford, the Bunting Institute at Radcliffe, and the Murphy Institute at Tulane University.

WILL KYMLICKA is Canada Research Chair in Political Philosophy, Department of Philosophy, Queen's University, Kingston, Ontario. He is a leading thinker regarding issues of nationalism, multiculturalism, and citizenship. His work has helped to shape the debate on the rights and status of ethnocultural groups in liberal democracies.

Kymlicka is the author of many books and articles and has edited numerous publications. His work has been translated into over twenty-five languages. His best-known books include *Contemporary Political Philosophy* (1990), *Finding Our Way: Rethinking Ethnocultural Relations in Canada* (1998), *Politics in the Vernacular: Nationalism, Multiculturalism and Citizenship* (2001), and *Multicultural Citizenship* (1995), which was awarded the C. B. MacPherson prize by the Canadian Political Science Association, and the Ralph J. Bunche award by the American Political Science Association, both in 1996.

Will Kymlicka received his B.A. in philosophy and politics in 1984 from Queen's University. He earned his B.Phil. in 1986 and Ph.D. in 1987, both from Oxford University. Since 1998, he has taught in the Department of Philosophy at Queen's University, and in the Nationalism Studies program at the Central European University in Budapest. Kymlicka has been a visiting scholar throughout Europe, Canada, and the United States since 1986. In 2003 he was named as a fellow of the Royal Society of Canada.

ROBERT POST is the David Boies Professor of Law at the Yale Law School. He specializes in constitutional theory and academic freedom. He is the author of *Constitutional Domains: Democracy, Community, Management*, the coauthor of *Prejudicial Appearances: The Logic of American Antidiscrimination Law*, the editor of *Censorship and Silencing: Practices of Cultural Regulation* and *Law and the Order of*

Culture, and the coeditor of *Civil Society and Government*, *Human Rights in Political Transitions: Gettysburg to Bosnia*, and *Race and Representation: Affirmative Action*.

JEREMY J. WALDRON is University Professor in the Law School at New York University. He is best known for his works in the area of overlap between jurisprudence, the theory of politics, and moral and political philosophy. He is most interested in liberal theories of rights, issues of economic and social justice, the political significance of moral disagreement, and the basis of our political ideals in a multicultural society.

Waldron's most recent books include *The Dignity of Legislation* (1999), *Law and Disagreement* (1999), and *God, Locke and Equality* (2002). He also is widely published in many law reviews and journals.

A native of New Zealand, Jeremy Waldron earned his B.A. in Otago, New Zealand, in 1974 and his LL.B in 1978. He received his D.Phil. in 1986 from Oxford University and an honorary Doctorate in Laws from the Catholic University of Brussels in 2003. He held lectureships in New Zealand, Oxford, and Scotland from 1975 to 1987 and was a professor at the Boalt Hall School of Law at the University of California, Berkeley from 1986 to 1996. He also held the position of associate dean and chair of the Jurisprudence and Social Policy Program at Berkeley from 1993 to 1994. Waldron served as University Professor at Columbia University from 2005 to 2006, and before that, from 1997 to 2004, he was the Maurice and Hilda Friedman Professor at Columbia Law School and director of Columbia's Center for Law and Philosophy. He is a member of the American Academy of Arts and Sciences.

Another Cosmopolitanism

Introduction

ROBERT POST

The conflagration of World War II made manifest the inescapable interdependence of the globe. For the past half century, we have grown ever more tightly interconnected by the expanding international circulation of persons, capital, commerce, pollution, information, labor, goods, viruses, and so on, *ad infinitum*. In the arresting images from space of our frail, robin's egg planet, we have been privileged to witness the unity that previous millennia could envision only by inhabiting the mind of God. The present question, the question taken up by Seyla Benhabib in this slim but significant volume, is how we can fashion political and legal institutions to govern ourselves, all together, on this earth.

For centuries, we have articulated issues of morality and ethics within a language of universalism. We have asked what we owe our fellow human beings, not what we owe our fellow-citizens. Exemplary is the "universalist moral standpoint" adopted by "the discourse theory of ethics" (18), of which Seyla Benhabib is such an eminent representative. The ordinary organization of our legal and political life, however, stands in sharp contrast to this ethical standpoint, for it does not contain an analogous universalist tradition. To the contrary, as Benhabib writes, we have long believed that "[p]olitical actors need bounded communities—whether they be cities, regions, states, or transnational institutions—within which they can establish mechanisms of representation, accountability, participation, and deliberation" (Reply 169). Ever since the Enlightenment we have conceptualized law as legitimate only insofar as it expresses a political will that has been forged within the walled fora of these bounded communities.

If the universalism of our ethics ultimately derives from commitments to the transcendent and equal dignity of all persons, the particularism of our law ultimately derives from the well-guarded borders of our states. We face two difficulties in attempting to imagine law that does not root itself in the circumscribed polis of a state. The first is that law must be binding, not merely advisory. We typically take this to mean that law must be enforceable, which presupposes administrative institutions, such as courts or police, that are charged with the responsibility of enforcing law. We have great difficulty imagining how such institutions might exist apart from discrete states.

The second and deeper difficulty is that law must be authoritative. Because contemporary law can not easily appeal to the authority of God, nature, divine rulers, or universal ethics, it must instead appeal to the authority of democratic self-determination. But democracies always create law, whether through legislatures or courts, in the name of some specifically defined and bounded group of persons, who constitute a people that purports to govern itself. In the absence of a single worldwide republic, humanity must remain splintered into competing and divided democratically self-governing peoples. These divisions necessarily belie aspirations for a universal democratic law.

Human rights, which seek to protect human beings as persons rather than as citizens of particular states, nevertheless purport to embody a law that is cosmopolitan and international and that does not depend for authority on the democratic will of particular states. The astonishingly rapid rise of human rights conventions and agreements in the years after Nuremberg has thus sharpened tensions between the particularity of positive law, which is characteristically endowed with authority and enforceability by the institutions of specific states, and the universality of ethical obligations, which are conceived as owed to each and every person regardless of the contingent vagaries of positive state law. Human rights aspire to embody universal ethical obligations within the form of law.

Technically proficient lawyers are unsettled by this aspiration. They typically attribute the authority of human rights law to treaties, which are agreements among states, or to the contingent fact that domestic legal systems have positively consented to incorporate human rights principles into municipal law, from sources that are either domestic or international. Those not dedicated to the technical niceties of the law, however, know full well that the force and appeal of human rights now far exceed these narrow jurisprudential foundations. In the popular mind, human rights have assumed a discursive authority that is plainly legal, and even within professional circles, as contemporary debates over the status of international customary law suggest, they hover ambiguously in the fraught space that separates ethics from legality. A fundamental challenge for our time is the construction of a jurisprudential theory able to reconcile the universality of human rights with the partiality of positive law.

Benhabib perceives the urgency of this challenge, and in this volume she rises to address it primarily by focusing on the human rights of persons who reside within a state but who are excluded from its polity—legal and illegal aliens. Benhabib asks whether such persons are protected by a law that is superior to the positive law of a state, a law that can bend "the will of sovereign nations" (16). She crafts her answer by drawing on Kant's doctrine of cosmopolitan rights, which she attributes to Kant's thesis that "The Law of World Citizenship Shall be Limited to Conditions of Universal Hospitality." Benhabib interprets the law of hospitality to cover the relationship between states and strangers. Because Kant (and Benhabib) also believe that the domestic law of a state should be republican, the law of hospitality necessarily intersects with the democratic authority of ordinary positive law.

Benhabib's striking and original contribution is carefully to attend precisely to this point of intersection. She notes that democracies (by definition) possess transparent public spheres that are designed to translate the ethical views of citizens into the positive law of the state. And she also notes the growing "democratic forces within global civil society" (71) that are ethically committed to the idea that legal and illegal aliens should be accorded basic human rights.

Joining together these two observations, Benhabib postulates a "project of mediations" (20) through which cosmopolitan norms come to acquire positive legal status. Put briefly and schematically, Benhabib argues that the transparency of democratic states allows citizens to become increasingly convinced of the independent validity of cosmopolitan norms, and that as a consequence citizens can "*reiterate* these principles and incorporate them into democratic will-formation processes through argument, contestation, revision and rejection" (49). Benhabib's profound insight is to conceptualize the emergence of cosmopolitan law as a dynamic process through which the principles of human rights are progressively incorporated into the positive law of democratic states.

Benhabib calls this process "democratic iteration," which she conceives as involving a "jurisgenerative politics" that mediates "between universal norms and the will of democratic majorities" (49). Democratic iteration functions at two levels. It alters the substance of democratic law, so that the content of democratic law is progressively reconstructed along lines that reflect principles of ethical universalism. And it also alters the very boundaries by which democratic states are defined. Although all "democracies require borders" (33), because every democracy must define with specificity who may vote and who may not, these boundaries are fixed by positive law and are therefore subject to the force of democratic iteration.

Using the term "demos" to describe the citizens and voters who are authorized to determine the content of democratic law, Benhabib argues that the force of democratic iteration will push positive law to alter and expand the definition of the demos to include persons, such as legal and illegal aliens, who are subject to the jurisdiction of state law but who are not currently included within the demos. Benhabib illustrates this phenomenon by discussing developments in the European Union, where citizens of one member state can now vote in the local elections of other member states. She also observes it in the remarkable expansion of German citizenship and of persons entitled to vote in local German elections.

Benhabib teaches us that the contradiction between the universalism of ethics and the particularity of law can never be fully transcended but only progressively ameliorated in time. This is an insight of the first order. Benhabib does not, however, theorize why we may expect demoi increasingly to internalize cosmopolitan norms. Her confidence seems to rest on the idea that universal ethical norms are intrinsically valid, and so in the long run likely to be accepted. But this perspective is in some tension with Benhabib's acknowledgment that "Democratic rule and the claims of justice may contradict one another" (32). As those of us who suffer under American foreign policy well know, democratic majorities not infrequently ignore elementary ethical principles. Benhabib fully realizes that international law is not moving along steel tracks leading inevitably toward some guaranteed outcome.

In his comments on Benhabib's Lectures, therefore, Jeremy Waldron seeks to elucidate why we might have some confidence in the future emergence and internalization of cosmopolitan norms. Observing the increasing interdependence of nations and the rising levels of international trade and commerce, Waldron directs our attention to "the dense detail of ordinary life in which people routinely act and interact as though their dealings were conducted within some sort of ordered framework" (94). He suggests that cosmopolitan norms, the inclusion of aliens within norms of reciprocity and respect, might emerge from "the accretion and gradual crystallization of materials such as these" (96). "If we really want to understand how the world is coming to be ordered by cosmopolitan norms," Waldron explains, "we have to look at the ordinary as well as the extraordinary, the tedious as well as the exciting, the commercial as well as the ideological" (97). Waldron postulates that the democratic authority of such norms can reside as much "in the demotic dailiness" of "use and iterated modification" (97), as in the niceties of formal legal enactment.

In her Reply, Benhabib sharply disassociates herself from Waldron's vision. Without offering an alternative account of why democratic iterations will come to incorporate rather than repudiate cosmopolitans norms, she writes that "'Mundane and repeated contact' among different human groups is absolutely no guarantee of the spread of a cosmopolitan point of view that considers all human beings as individuals equally entitled to certain rights" (Reply 153). Benhabib is also concerned to insist that cosmopolitan norms can be fully instantiated only when they are embodied in "national legislation" (Reply 155). Her ambition is to ameliorate the tension between universalist ethics and the naked force of the state, as embodied in its positive law.

Benhabib's commitment to domestic law becomes most fully apparent in her response to Bonnie Honig. Honig urges that we view emerging cosmopolitan "norms, laws, and institutions" in "the most relentlessly political and critical terms" (104). She regards the tension between universalism and particularity as fundamental, so that international institutions that claim to enforce human rights and cosmopolitan norms "do not dispense with the need for membership; they just change the venue of membership" (107). Honig invites us to conclude that these institutions do not exemplify an extrapolitical universalist ethics, but challenge universalism at a different level and with a different agenda. She notes that "when claims to national belonging, say, in France, are being made by non-Europeans, the political (re)formation of Europe as a site of belonging is surely a way to resecure and not just attenuate or transcend national belonging" (114). Honig is most opposed to Benhabib's exclusive and singular focus on "law, states, and state-like and interstate institutions," which, although necessary, are nevertheless our "guardians, ventriloquizers, impersonators, shapers and censors of our voice, our desires, our aspirations, our solidarities" (120). Honig accordingly calls for a politics of the "double gesture, in which the promises *and* risks of a particular conditional order of hospitality (and universalism or cosmopolitanism) are both named and confronted" (112).

In her Reply, Benhabib neither denies nor allays Honig's fears that the state, as well as the new international institutions that claim to enforce human rights, might spawn novel and unanticipated forms of injustice, particularly with respect to the disempowered and disenfranchised. But Benhabib does insist that we must nevertheless seize the state and require it to enact human rights legislation "precisely for the sake of those who most need its protection" (Reply 164). She asks why Honig might believe that a politics of the double gesture should *substitute for*, rather than *supplement*, an alternative political agenda that seeks to incorporate cosmopolitan norms into positive law.

If Waldron and Honig each criticizes Benhabib's commitment to positive law, Will Kymlicka interrogates her attachment to the nation-state. Kymicka writes that observers of the European Union (EU) have regarded the expansion of the demos from two distinct and antithetical perspectives: the transcendence of liberal nationhood and the "taming" of liberal nationhood. Those who adopt the first perspective hope that the developments in EU citizenship discussed by Benhabib are a step toward the elimination of nationhood and toward the construction of a cosmopolitan, stateless future. By contrast, those who adopt the second perspective hope that these developments are a step toward the integration of aliens into the status of full national citizenship, a step that would reaffirm traditional liberal nationhood.

Advocates of the first view believe that the particularity of the nation-state is dangerous and should be eradicated; advocates of the second view believe that the nation-state is desirable but needs to be tamed so as to ameliorate its excesses, most obviously manifest in the nation-state's history of suppressing indigenous peoples and aliens and of belligerently warring with its rivalrous neighbors. Kymlicka himself unequivocally endorses the second approach, for he believes that liberal nationhood "has been a remarkable success in ensuring democracy, individual rights, peace and security, and economic prosperity for an ever-increasing number of people" (129). He wants "to push Benhabib to clarify the link between democratic iterations regarding cosmopolitan norms and liberal nationhood" (133).

In her response to Kymlicka, Benhabib distances herself from the traditional nation-state, advocating instead a strategy of maximizing the disjunction "between nationhood and democratic peoplehood" (Reply 168). Modern nation-states typically rest on the social solidarity of an *ethnos*, which is "a community bound together by the power of shared fate, memories, solidarity and belonging" (65). The ethnos endows the legal construction of the state with the intangible unity of nationhood. In contrast to a demos, which possesses boundaries that can be stipulated and manipulated by positive law, an ethnos "does not permit free entry and exit" (65). For this reason, Benhabib regards the national solidarity of the ethnos as essentially contradicting the universalist ethical principles to which she is otherwise committed. In responding to Kymlicka, therefore, Benhabib invites us to consider a future in which "civil, social, and some political rights" are maximally unbundled "from national belonging" (Reply 171).

Benhabib's conception of this future is not fully specified, but at a minimum it involves separating the demos from the ethnos. Benhabib advocates a "renegotiation of the boundaries between ethnos and demos such that the core nation reconstitutes itself in more universalistic terms" (Reply 174). In practice, this means establishing forms of democratic authority that fly free from the historical specificity of national boundaries, so that democratic decision making "can be exercised at local and regional as well as supra- and transnational levels" (Reply 172).

Universal cosmopolitanism presently faces two barriers to its success. The first is the necessary boundedness of democratic authority, and the second is the historically specific forms of national solidarity represented by the ethnos. In her lectures, Benhabib regards the first of these barriers as intrinsic to the tension between law and ethics, and she argues that it cannot be escaped but only ameliorated by temporal mediation. In her response to Kymlicka, Benhabib suggests that the second of these barriers is contingent and defeasible. Although it seems true that law can claim authority and validity even in the absence of an ethnos, it is not clear the extent to which well-functioning states require the solidarity of an ethnos. This would appear to be a practical question, answerable only by experience, albeit an experience modified by the ongoing internalization of cosmopolitan norms. Benhabib intimates that states can dispense with ethnos because a substitute "language of universalistic solidarity" can be created through claims of "socioeconomic equality" (Reply 175).

It is clear from her response to her three commentators that Benhabib is determined to press the principles of cosmopolitanism to their fullest possible embodiment, and that she is willing to limit these principles only as is necessary to preserve democratic authority. To assess her vision, we must try to imagine what the world would be like if states were precluded from appealing to the solidarity of ethnos. My best guess is that in a world of pure democratic authority, without ethnos, the demos could be conceived only as a frictionless agglomeration, arbitrarily composed and recomposed, filling whatever form is required by the functional needs of distinct units of democratic decision making. My hunch is that Benhabib would admire such a world because it would exemplify, to the fullest extent possible, the virtues and obligations of hospitality.

I am convinced by Benhabib that cosmopolitanism can take us no further than this, because cosmopolitanism must inevitably collide with the boundaries required by democratic authority. Whether cosmopolitanism can take us even this far, however, remains questionable. Even after endless reiterations, human society seems to remain recalcitrantly divided. Perhaps this is because persons tend to inhabit solidarities produced by shared memories of time past and by anticipated achievements in time future. The ethnos may in fact be nothing more than the social embodiment of these temporal modalities, the social form of these orientations toward past and future. The question plainly requires further attention.

For the present, however, it is sufficient to experience with great pleasure the depth of Benhabib's original and stimulating lectures, illuminated by the candid, insightful, and provocative comments of Jeremy Waldron, Bonnie Honig, and Will Kymlicka.

Another Cosmopolitanism

SEYLA BENHABIB

The Philosophical Foundations
of Cosmopolitan Norms

The Eichmann Trial

It is December 12, 1960. Israeli secret agents have captured Adolf Eichmann and the Israeli government has declared its intention to put Eichmann on trial. Karl Jaspers writes to Hannah Arendt: "The Eichmann trial is unsettling ... because I am afraid Israel may come away from it looking bad no matter how objective the conduct of the trial.... Its significance is not in its being a legal trial but in its establishing of historical facts and serving as a reminder of those facts for humanity."[1] For the next several months, and eventually years, an exchange ensues between Hannah Arendt and her teacher and mentor, Karl Jaspers, about the legality or illegality of the Eichmann trial, about institutional jurisdiction and about the philosophical foundations of international law, and in particular of 'crimes against humanity.'

Arendt replies that she is not as pessimistic as Jaspers is about "the legal basis of the trial" (*Correspondence*, 414). Israel can argue that Eichmann had been indicted in the first trial in Nuremberg and escaped arrest. In capturing Eichmann, Israel was capturing an outlaw—a *hostis humani generis* (an enemy of the human race)—who had been condemned of 'crimes against humanity.' He should have appeared before the Nuremberg Court, but because there was no successor court to carry out its mission, Arendt thinks that Israeli courts have a plausible basis for assuming jurisdiction.[2]

According to Hannah Arendt, *genocide* is the one crime that truly deserves the title 'crime against humanity.'[3] "Had the court in Jerusalem," she writes, "understood that there were distinctions between discrimination, expulsion, and genocide, it would have become clear that the supreme crime it was confronted with, the physical extermination of the Jewish people, was a crime against humanity, perpetrated upon the body of the Jewish people . . ." (*Eichmann* 1963, 269).

If, however, there are crimes which can be perpetrated against humanity itself, Arendt must consider the human being not only as a being worthy of moral respect but also as having a legal status that ought to be protected by international law. The distinguishing feature of this legal status is that it would take precedence over all existing legal orders and it would bind them (*Correspondence*, 419). *Crimes against humanity* are different than other crimes, which can only exist when there is a known and promulgated law that has been violated.[4] Which are the laws that crimes against humanity violate, particularly if, as in the case of Eichmann and the Nazi genocide of the Jews, a state and its established legal system sanctify genocide, and even order it to be committed? A crime, as distinct from a moral injury, cannot be defined independently of posited law and a positive legal order.[5]

Arendt is aware that on account of philosophical perplexities, there will be a tendency to think of crimes against humanity as "crimes against humanness" or "humaneness," as if what was intended was a moral injury that violated some kind of shared moral code. The Nuremberg Charter's definition of crimes against humanity (*Verbrechen gegen die Menschheit*) was translated into German as "crimes against humaneness" (*Verbrechen gegen die Menschlichkeit*), "as if," she observes, "the Nazis had simply been lacking in human kindness, certainly the understatement of the century" (*Eichmann* 1963, 275; *Correspondence*, 423, 431).

Although Jaspers is willing to accept Arendt's distinction between *crimes against humanity* versus *humaneness*, he points out that since international law and natural law are not "law in the same sense that underlies normal court proceedings" (*Correspondence*, 424), it would be most appropriate for Israel to transfer the competency to judge Eichmann either to the UN, to the International Court at the Hague, or to courts provided for by the UN Charter.

Neither Arendt nor Jaspers harbors any illusions, however, that the UN General Assembly would rise up to this task (Eichmann 1963, 270). The Postscript to *Eichmann in Jerusalem* ends on an unexpected and surprising note: "It is quite conceivable that certain political responsibilities among nations might some day be adjudicated in an international court; what is inconceivable is that such a court would be a criminal tribunal which pronounces on the guilt or innocence of individuals" (*Eichmann* 1963, 298).

Why does Arendt deny that an International Criminal Court is conceivable? Does she mean that it is unlikely to come into existence, or rather that, even if it were to come into existence, it would be without authority? Her position is all the more baffling because her very insistence on the juridical as opposed to the merely moral dimension of crimes against humanity suggests the need for a standing international body that would possess the jurisdiction to try such crimes committed by individuals.

We encounter here a perplexity the significance of which goes well beyond the consistency or lack thereof in Arendt's views on international law. Although both Jaspers and Arendt are Kantians and are deeply indebted to the cosmopolitan legacy of Kantian thought, Arendt is more of a civic republican, or maybe even a political existentialist,[6] than Jaspers is. Arendt, although a Kantian in moral theory, remains committed to a civic republican vision of political self-determination.

Cosmopolitan Norms of Justice

The Eichmann trial, much like the Nuremberg trials before it, captured some of the perplexities of the emerging norms of cosmopolitan justice. It will be my thesis that since the UN Declaration of Human Rights in 1948, we have entered a phase in the evolution of global civil society, which is characterized by a transition from *international* to *cosmopolitan* norms of justice. Norms of international justice most commonly arise through treaty obligations and bilateral or multilateral agreements among states and their representatives. They regulate relations among states and other principals that are authorized to act as the agents of states in multiple domains, ranging from trade and commerce to war and security, the environment, and the media.

Cosmopolitan norms of justice, whatever the conditions of their legal origination, accrue to individuals as moral and legal persons in a worldwide civil society. Even if cosmopolitan norms arise through treatylike obligations, such as the UN Charter can be considered to be for the signatory states, their peculiarity is that they endow *individuals* rather than states and their agents with certain rights and claims. This is the uniqueness of the many human rights agreements signed since World War II. They signal an eventual transition from a model of international law based on treaties among states to cosmopolitan law understood as international public law that binds and bends the will of sovereign nations.[7]

In contemporary debates, terms such as 'globalization' and 'empire' are often used to capture these transformations. Yet these terms are misleading in that they fail to address the distinctiveness of cosmopolitan norms. Defenders of globalization who view it as primarily an economic phenomenon reduce cosmopolitan norms to a thin version of the human rights to life, liberty, equality, and property, which are supposed to accompany the spread of free markets and trading practices. Theorists of empire, most notably, Michael Hardt and Antonio Negri, distinguish between *imperialism* and *empire* in order to capture the logic of the new international order.[8] Whereas imperialism refers to a predatory, extractive, and exploitative order through which one or more sovereign power imposes its will on others, 'empire' is said to refer to an anonymous network of rules, regulations, and structures that entrap one in the system of global capitalism. Global capitalism is accompanied by legal norms that not

only protect and enable capitalist property relations but also that regulate the technological, communicative, informational, and security
infrastructures of capitalism. Empire is a hegemon without a center.

Whether it is the *thin* version of globalization as presented in the
work of free marketeers or the *thicker* version as presented in that of
theorists of empire, each fails to capture the challenge of cosmopolitan
norms in the present. Although the evolution of cosmopolitan norms
of justice is a tremendous development, the relationship between the
spread of cosmopolitan norms and democratic self-determination is
fraught, both theoretically and politically. How can the will of democratic majorities be reconciled with norms of cosmopolitan justice?
How can legal norms and standards, which originate outside the will of
democratic legislatures, become binding on them? To examine this
fraught relationship will be the task of these essays.

In this chapter, I engage in a complex dialogue with Arendt, Jaspers,
and Kant (II and III). The distinguishing feature of the period we are
in cannot be captured through the *bon mots* of 'globalization' and
'empire'; rather, we are also facing the rise of an international human
rights regime and the spread of cosmopolitan norms, while the relationship between state sovereignty and such norms is becoming more
contentious and conflictual (IV). Such conflicts render starkly visible
the 'paradox of democratic legitimacy,' namely, the necessary and
inevitable limitation of democratic forms of representation and
accountability in terms of the formal distinction between members
and nonmembers (V). This is the core tension, even if not contradiction, between democratic self-determination and the norms of cosmopolitan justice.

Cosmopolitanism and Discursive Scope

The term 'cosmopolitanism,' along with 'empire' and 'globalization,'
has become one of the keywords of our times. For some, cosmopolitanism signifies an attitude of enlightened morality that does not place

'love of country' ahead of 'love of mankind' (Martha Nussbaum); for others, cosmopolitanism signifies hybridity, fluidity, and recognizing the fractured and internally riven character of human selves and citizens, whose complex aspirations cannot be circumscribed by national fantasies and primordial communities (Jeremy Waldron). For a third group of thinkers, whose lineages are those of Critical Theory, cosmopolitanism is a normative philosophy for carrying the universalistic norms of discourse ethics beyond the confines of the nation-state (Juergen Habermas, David Held, and James Bohman).[9]

My project is most aligned with the aspirations of this latter group. But in recent debates the question of 'discursive scope' has not been given serious consideration. In extending the norms of discourse ethics toward a cosmopolitan political philosophy, Held and Bohman in particular have not addressed the paradox of bounded communities. Here I part company from my Critical Theory colleagues and join in the anxiety expressed by Arendt's puzzling observations about an International Criminal Court. I do so, not because I agree with Arendt, but because I believe that this anxiety must be faced by any serious deliberative democrat.

What is meant by discursive scope?[10] Because the discourse theory of ethics articulates a universalist moral standpoint, it cannot limit the scope of the *moral conversation* only to those who reside within nationally recognized boundaries; it views the moral conversation as potentially including all of *humanity*. Put sharply, every person, and every moral agent, who has interests and whom my actions and the consequences of my actions can impact and affect in some manner or another is potentially a moral conversation partner with me: I have a moral obligation to *justify my actions with reasons* to this individual or to the representatives of this being. I respect the moral worth of the other by recognizing that I must provide him or her with a justification for my actions. We are all potential participants in such conversations of justification.

Due to the open-endedness of discourses of moral justification, there will be an inevitable and necessary tension between those moral obligations and duties resulting from our membership in bounded communities and the moral perspective that we must adopt as human beings *simpliciter*. From a universalist and cosmopolitan point of view, however, boundaries, including state borders and frontiers, require moral justification. The stipulations of discourse ethics to consider each and every human being as a moral agent with whom I can share a conversation of justification cannot be applied to the domain of political membership without the aid of further premises, nor is it necessary to do so. A discursive approach should place *significant limitations* on what can count as *morally permissible* practices of inclusion and exclusion within sovereign polities.

This confronts the discourse theorist with a dilemma: a shared feature of all norms of membership including, but not only, norms of citizenship is that those who are affected by the consequences of these norms and, in the first place, by criteria of exclusion, *per definitionem* cannot be party to their articulation. Membership norms impact those who are not members precisely by distinguishing insiders from outsiders, citizens from noncitizens. This then gives rise to a dilemma: either a discourse theory is simply *irrelevant* to membership practices in bounded communities in that it cannot articulate *any* justifiable criteria of exclusion, or it simply *accepts* existing practices of exclusion as *morally neutral* historical contingencies that require no further validation. This would suggest that a discourse theory of democracy is itself chimerical insofar as democracy requires a morally justifiable closure that discourse ethics cannot deliver.

Unlike communitarians who reduce the demands of morality to those claims that are deemed valid by specific ethical, cultural and political communities, and unlike realists and postmodernists who are skeptical that political norms can ever be judged in the light of moral ones, I will insist *on the necessary disjunction as well as the necessary mediation between the moral and the ethical, the moral and the political*. The task is one of mediations, not reductions. How can one mediate moral universalism with ethical particularism? How can one mediate legal and political norms with moral ones? Such a strategy of mediation is crucial to reclaiming dialogic universalism.

Cosmopolitanism then is a philosophical project of mediations, not of reductions or of totalizations. Cosmopolitanism is not equivalent to a global ethic as such; nor is it adequate to characterize cosmopolitanism through cultural attitudes and choices alone. I follow the Kantian tradition in thinking of cosmopolitanism as the emergence of norms that ought to govern relations among individuals in a global civil society. These norms are neither merely moral nor just legal. They may best be characterized as framing the 'morality of the law,' but in a global rather than a domestic context. They signal the eventual legalization and juridification of the rights claims of human beings everywhere, regardless of their membership in bounded communities. Membership in bounded communities, which may be smaller or larger than territorially defined nation-states, remains nevertheless crucial.

Kant's Cosmopolitan Legacy

The Eichmann trial and the Arendt-Jaspers exchange surrounding it are interesting precisely because they stand at the beginning of the evolution of cosmopolitan norms, the full implications of which have only become clear in our time. To appreciate Arendt's and Jaspers's positions, as well as the differences among them, it is necessary to examine briefly Kant's doctrine of cosmopolitan right. Arendt and Jaspers are grappling with a Kantian legacy: neither accepts legal positivism or natural law.[11] According to legal positivism, the legal system is a conceptual and juridical hierarchy in which norms refer to other norms. Any criticism voiced against this system, invoking criteria other than those permitted by the logic of legal argumentation, evaluation, and debate, relies on norms that transcend the logic of legality.[12] The moral critique of legality presents an "extralegal" moment, alien to the logic of the law, unless the sovereign endows morality itself with the force of law.

After the experiences of the Third Reich and Nazi dictatorship, Arendt and Jaspers have no illusions that the legal system can serve as its own moral foundation; yet philosophically as well as historically, they consider natural law doctrines to be obsolete. They believe that to postulate a fixed human nature, as natural law doctrines do, is to fall into a metaphysics of substance and to view the human being as an entity. Following Heidegger's insight that *Dasein* is the only being for whom the question of its existence is meaningful, they prefer the language of "human *Existenz*" or of the "human condition" to that of human nature.[13] The human condition refers to those circumstances under which life is given to human beings. These circumstances constrain our choices, but nevertheless we are free to choose our fate. Yet if natural law is not defensible, and legal positivism is morally suspect, how can one give meaning to concepts such as 'crimes against humanity'?[14] Kant's doctrine of cosmopolitan right shows the way here.

The conceptual innovation of Kant's doctrine of cosmopolitanism is that Kant recognized three interrelated but distinct levels of 'right,' in the juridical senses of the term.[15] First is domestic law, the sphere of posited relations of right, which Kant claims should be in accordance with a republican constitution; second is the sphere of rightful relations among nations (*Voelkerrecht*), resulting from treaty obligations among states; third is cosmopolitan right, which concerns relations among civil persons to each other as well as to organized political entities in a global civil society.[16]

Kant introduces the term *"Weltbuergerrecht"* (cosmopolitan right) in the Third Article of "Perpetual Peace," with reference to the duty of hospitality.[17] The duty of hospitality is of interest because it touches on the quintessential case of an individual coming into contact with an organized and bounded political entity. The German reads: "Das Weltbuergerrecht soll auf Bedingungen der allgemeinen Hospitalitaet eingeschraenkt sein" or *"The Law of World Citizenship Shall be Limited to Conditions of Universal Hospitality"* (Kant [1795] 1923, 443). Kant himself notes the oddity of the locution "hospitality" in this context, and therefore remarks that "it is not a question of philanthropy but of right." In other words, *hospitality* is not to be understood as a virtue of sociability, as the kindness and generosity one may show to strangers who come to one's land or who become dependent on one's act of kindness through circumstances of nature or history; hospitality is a right that belongs to all human beings insofar as we view them as potential participants in a world republic. Following Kant, Arendt likewise argues that 'crimes against humanity' are not violations of moral norms alone, but violations of the rights of humanity in our person. Are these moral or juridical rights? Let us look more closely.

According to Kant, the right of hospitality entails a claim to temporary residency on the part of the stranger who comes on our land. This cannot be refused, if such refusal would involve the *destruction*—Kant's word here is *"Untergang"*—of the stranger. To refuse sojourn to victims of religious wars, to victims of piracy or ship-wreckage, when such refusal would lead to their demise, is untenable. What remains unclear in Kant's discussion is whether such relations among peoples and nations involve acts of supererogation, which go beyond the reasonable demands of morality into the realm of altruism, or whether they entail a moral claim pertaining to the rights of humanity in the person of the other.

The right of hospitality is situated at the boundaries of the polity; it delimits civic space by regulating relations among members, strangers and bounded communities. It occupies that space between human rights and civil and political rights, between the rights of humanity in our person and the rights that accrue to us insofar as we are citizens of specific republics.

We may identify here the juridical and moral ambivalence that affects discussions of the right of asylum and refuge to this day. Are the rights of asylum and refuge rights in the sense of being *reciprocal moral obligations* that, in some sense or another, are grounded on our mutual humanity? Or are these rights claims in the narrow legal sense of being *enforceable norms* of behavior that individuals and groups can hold each other obliged to obey, and, in particular, force sovereign nation-states to comply with? Kant's discussion provides no clear answer. The right of hospitality entails a moral claim with potential legal consequences, in that the obligation of the receiving states to grant temporary residency to foreigners is anchored in a republican cosmopolitical order. Such an order does not have a supreme executive law governing it. In this sense, the obligation to show hospitality to foreigners and strangers cannot be enforced; it remains a voluntarily incurred obligation on the part of the political sovereign. The right of hospitality expresses the dilemmas of a republican cosmopolitical order in a nutshell: how to create quasi-legally binding obligations through voluntary commitments and in the absence of an overwhelming sovereign power with the ultimate right of enforcement?

By delineating a conceptual space between universal norms of morality and positive law with respect to the actions and interactions of individuals in the world community—Kant uses the locution "*der Erdkugel*" (the globe) to characterize this space—Kant laid the foundations for a post-Westphalian legal order. Kant's "Perpetual Peace" essay signaled a watershed between two conceptions of sovereignty and paved the way for the transition from the first to the second. We can name these "Westphalian sovereignty" and "liberal international sovereignty."[18] In the classical Westphalian regime of sovereignty states are free and equal; they enjoy ultimate authority over all objects and subjects within a circumscribed territory; relations with other sovereigns are voluntary and contingent; these relations are limited in kind and scope to transitory military and economic alliances as well as cultural and religious affinities; above all, states "regard cross-border processes as a 'private matter' concerning only those immediately affected."[19]

By contrast, according to conceptions of liberal international sovereignty the formal equality of states increasingly is dependent on their subscribing to common values and principles, such as the observance of human rights, the rule of law, and respect for democratic self-determination. Sovereignty no longer means ultimate and arbitrary authority over a circumscribed territory; states which treat their citizens in violation of certain norms, close their borders, prevent freedoms of market, speech, and association and the like are thought not to belong within a specific society of states or alliances; the anchoring of domestic principles in institutions shared with others is crucial. In Michael Ignatieff's words, this mode of sovereignty is subject to the "naming and shaming" processes of civil and cultural sanctions, which, although not forcing states to comply militarily, nonetheless can influence their behavior.[20]

Although the subjects of international law were historically states and organized political entities, cosmopolitan norms go beyond liberal international sovereignty by envisaging a conceptual and juridical space for a domain of rights-relations that would be binding on *nonstate actors* as well as on *state actors* when they come into contact with individuals who are not members of their own polities. Kant envisaged a world in which all members of the human race eventually would became participants in a civil order and enter into a condition of lawful association with one another. Yet this civil condition of lawful coexistence was not equivalent to membership in a republican polity. In an extremely important move, Kant argued that cosmopolitan citizens still needed their individual republics to be citizens at all. This is why he so carefully distinguished a "world government" from a "world federation." A "world government" would only result in a "universal monarchy," he argued, and would be a "soulless despotism," whereas a federative union (*eine foederative Vereinigung*) would still permit the exercise of citizenship within bounded communities (Kant [1795] 1923, 453).

Concepts such as 'the right to universal hospitality,' 'crimes against humanity,' 'the right to have rights' (Arendt) are the legacy of Kantian cosmopolitanism. In each instance, they articulate a shared philosophical perplexity: Kant, Arendt, and Jaspers want to give these concepts a binding power over and beyond the moral obligation which they impose on individual agents. These concepts should not be treated as mere "oughts"; they must generate enforceable norms not only for individuals but for collective actors as well, and in the first place, for states and governments. The right to universal hospitality, for example, if it means anything at all, imposes an obligation on the political sovereign, by prohibiting states from denying refuge and asylum to those whose intentions are peaceful and if refusing them sojourn would result in their demise. The 'right to have rights,' in Arendt's memorable formulation,[21] prohibits states from *denaturalizing* individuals by denying them citizenship rights and state protection. The concept of 'crimes against humanity' expressly prohibits government officials, state bureaucrats and others in positions of power from acting in such a way as to engage in "murder, extermination, enslavement, deportation, and other inhumane acts committed against any civilian population, before or during war; or persecution on political, racial or religious grounds ... whether or not in violation of domestic law of the country where perpetrated."[22] These categories are intended to provide not only precepts of individual conduct but also principles of public morality and institutional justice. They transcend the specific positive laws of any existing legal order by formulating binding norms which no promulgated legislation ought to violate. What then is the philosophical puzzle concerning cosmopolitan norms? I will distinguish among three different issues here:

- First, there are questions concerning the philosophical foundations of cosmopolitan rights claims. Certainly, before Kant the Western legal tradition recognized a sphere of international law that went beyond specific treaty obligations concluded by various sovereigns. Stoic conceptions of natural law, Roman conceptions of *jus gentium* (the law of nations), and Christian conceptions of the law of the Christian commonwealth established guidelines for nations in their dealings with one another.[23] Kant relied on the work of other natural law thinkers before him, such as Pufendorf, Grotius, and Vattel.[24] But how could one justify *cosmopolitan right* without falling back on some conception of a fixed human nature or a shared system of religious belief? What, if any, are the ontological foundations of cosmopolitan right after Kantian critical philosophy?

- Second, cosmopolitan right, if it is to deserve its name at all, must bind, that is, must guide as well as be enforceable on, the actions and the will of sovereign legal and political entities. Cosmopolitan right trumps positive law, although there is no higher sovereign authority that is authorized to enforce it. What is the authority of norms that themselves are not backed by a higher authority, either in the conceptual sense or in the sense of enforcement?

- Third, Kant, Arendt, and Jaspers, although anticipating a world society governed by cosmopolitan norms of justice, also proceed from the premise of a "divided" mankind that is organized into discrete, self-determining, and sovereign political entities. At times, this is a concession to political realism on their part; more often though, and particularly for Kant and Arendt, the division of humankind into self-governing polities is not a *factum brutum* but has a value in itself. Whereas Jaspers is ultimately willing to abdicate republican self-governance and entertain the possibility of world government,[25] neither Kant nor Arendt can reconcile world government with the values of private and public autonomy. Therefore, the tension between the demands of cosmopolitan justice and the values of republican self-governance is greatest in their work.

I will address these philosophical puzzles by discussing them in reverse order. I will proceed from an analysis of the tension between cosmopolitan norms and republican self-governance (3) to the matter of the authority of cosmopolitan norms (2) and finally arrive at the ontological puzzle (1). My concern is less with the kind of ontological universe in which cosmopolitan norms can be said to exist, than with how these norms, whatever their ontological status, can shape, guide, and constrain our political life, by creating new spaces for evaluative articulation and by extending our political imagination.

The Rise of an International Human Rights Regime

Kant, Arendt, and Jaspers anticipated and intimated the evolution of cosmopolitan norms of justice. In the intervening years, institutional developments have led us to frame certain questions differently, whereas others can still very much be understood in terms of puzzles they identified. What are these institutional developments? Since the 1948 Universal Declaration of Human Rights, an international human rights regime has emerged. By an 'international human rights regime,' I understand a set of interrelated and overlapping global and regional regimes that encompass human rights treaties as well as customary international law or international soft law.[26]

The rise of multiple human rights regimes causes both collusion and confluence between international and domestic law. The consequence is a complex system of interdependence that gives the lie to Carl Schmitt's dictum that "there is no sovereign to force the sovereign."[27] As Gerald Neuman observes, "National constitutions vary greatly in their provisions regarding the relationship between international and domestic law. Some are more or less dualist, treating international norms as part of a distinct legal system. . . . Others are more or less monist, treating international law and domestic law as a single legal system, often giving some category of international norms legal supremacy over domestic legislation."[28] This transformation of human rights codes into generalizable norms that ought to govern the behavior of sovereign states is one of the most promising aspects of contemporary political globalization processes.

We are witnessing this development in at least three related areas:

i. *Crimes against Humanity, Genocide, and War Crimes*. The concept of *crimes against humanity*, first articulated by the Allied powers in the Nuremberg trials of Nazi war criminals, stipulates that there are certain norms in accordance with which state officials as well as private individuals are to treat one another, even, and precisely under, conditions of extreme hostility and war. Ethnic cleansing, mass executions, rape, cruel and unusual punishment of the enemy, such as dismemberment, which occur under conditions of a "widespread or systematic attack" are proscribed and can all constitute sufficient grounds for the indictment and prosecution of individuals who are responsible for these actions, even if they are or were state officials, or subordinates who acted under orders. The refrain of the soldier and the bureaucrat—"I was only doing my duty"—is no longer an acceptable ground for abrogating the rights of humanity in the person of the other, even when, and especially when, the other is your enemy.

During the Nuremberg trials, crimes against humanity referred to crimes committed during *international* armed conflicts.[29] Immediately after the Nuremberg trials, *genocide* also was included as a crime against humanity but was left distinct due its own jurisdictional status which was codified in Article II of the Convention on the Prevention and Punishment of the Crime of Genocide (1948). *Genocide* is the knowing and willful destruction of the way of life and existence of a collectivity whether through acts of total war, racial extinction, or ethnic cleansing. It is the supreme crime against humanity, in that it aims at the destruction of human variety, of the many and diverse ways of being human. Genocide not only eliminates individuals who may belong to this or another group; it aims at the extinction of their way of life.[30]

By contrast, *war crimes*, as defined in the Statute of the International Criminal Tribunal for the Former Yugoslavia (1993), initially only applied to *international conflicts*. With the Statute of the International Criminal Tribunal for Rwanda (1994), recognition was extended to *internal armed conflict* as well. 'War crimes' now refer to international as well as internal conflicts that involve the mistreatment or abuse of civilians and noncombatants as well as one's enemy in combat.[31]

Thus, in a significant development since World War II, crimes against humanity, genocide, and war crimes have all been extended to apply not only to atrocities that take place in international conflict situations but to events *within* the borders of a sovereign country that may be perpetrated by officials of that country or by its citizens during peacetime as well.

The continuing rearticulation of these three categories in international law, and in particular their extension from situations of international armed conflict to civil wars within a country and to the actions of governments against their own people, has in turn encouraged the emergence of the concept of 'humanitarian interventions.'

ii. *Humanitarian Interventions.* The theory and practice of humanitarian interventions was appealed to by the United States and its North Atlantic Treaty Organization (NATO) allies in order to justify their actions against ethnic cleansing and continuing crimes against the civilian population in Bosnia and Kosovo. Although lacking clear guidelines in international law and the UN Charter, humanitarian interventions are based on the belief that when a sovereign nation-state egregiously violates the basic human rights of a segment of its population on account of its religion, race, ethnicity, language, or culture there is a *generalized moral obligation* to end actions such as genocide and crimes against humanity.[32] In such cases, human rights norms trump state sovereignty claims. No matter how controversial in interpretation and application they may be, humanitarian interventions are based on the growing consensus that the sovereignty of the state to dispose of the life, liberty, and property of its citizens or residents is not unconditional or unlimited.[33] State sovereignty is no longer the ultimate arbiter of the fate of citizens or residents. The exercise of state sovereignty even within domestic borders is increasingly subject to internationally recognized norms that prohibit genocide, ethnocide, mass expulsions, enslavement, rape, and forced labor.

iii. *Transnational Migration.* The third area in which international human rights norms are creating binding guidelines upon the will of sovereign nation-states is that of international migration. *Humanitarian interventions* deal with the treatment by nation-states of their citizens or residents; *crimes against humanity* and *war crimes* concern relations among enemies or opponents in nationally bounded as well as extraterritorial settings. *Transnational migrations*, by contrast, pertain to the rights of individuals, not insofar as they are considered members of concrete bounded communities but insofar as they are human beings *simpliciter*, when they come into contact with, seek entry into, or want to become members of territorially bounded communities.

The Universal Declaration of Human Rights recognizes the right to freedom of movement across boundaries—a right to emigrate—that is to leave a country, but not a right to immigrate, a right to enter a country (Article 13). Article 14 anchors the right to enjoy asylum under certain circumstances, whereas Article 15 of the Declaration proclaims that everyone has "the right to a nationality." The second half of Article 15 stipulates that "No one shall be arbitrarily deprived of his nationality nor denied the right to change his nationality."[34]

Yet the Universal Declaration is silent on states' *obligations* to grant entry to immigrants, to uphold the right of asylum, and to permit citizenship to residents and denizens. These rights have no specific addressees and they do not appear to anchor *specific* obligations on the part of second and third parties to comply with them. Despite the cross-border character of these rights, the Declaration upholds the sovereignty of individual states. Thus, a series of internal contradictions between universal human rights and territorial sovereignty are built into the logic of the most comprehensive international law document in our world.

The Geneva Convention of 1951 relating to the Status of Refugees and its Protocol added in 1967 is the second most important international legal document after the Universal Declaration. Nevertheless, neither the existence of this document nor the creation of the United Nations High Commissioner on Refugees has altered the fact that this Convention and its Protocol are binding on signatory states alone and can be brazenly disregarded by nonsignatories and, at times, even by signatory states themselves. Some lament the fact that as international human rights norms are increasingly invoked in immigration, refugee and asylum disputes, territorially delimited nations are challenged not only in their claims to control their borders but also in their prerogative to define the boundaries of the national community. Others criticize the Universal Human Rights Declaration for not endorsing institutional cosmopolitanism, and for upholding an "interstatal" rather than a truly cosmopolitan international order.[35] Yet one thing is clear: the treatment by states of citizens and residents within their boundaries is no longer an unchecked prerogative. One of the cornerstones of Wetsphalian sovereignty, namely that states enjoy ultimate authority over all objects and subjects within their circumscribed territory, has been delegitimized through international law. I concur with David Held that cosmopolitan justice "conceives of international law as a system of public law. . . . Cosmopolitan sovereignty is the law of peoples because it places at its center the primacy of individual human beings as political agents, and the accountability of power."[36]

The evolution of cosmopolitan norms, however, is rife with a central contradiction: although territorially bounded states are increasingly subject to international norms, states themselves are the principal signatories as well as enforcers of the multiple human rights treaties and conventions through which international norms spread. In this process, the state is both sublated and reinforced in its authority. Throughout the international system, as long as territorially bounded states are recognized as the sole legitimate units of negotiation and representation, a tension, and at times even a fatal contradiction, is palpable: the modern state system is caught between *sovereignty* and *hospitality*, between the prerogative to choose to be a party to cosmopolitan norms and human rights treaties, and the obligation to extend recognition of these human rights to all.

In a Kantian vein, by 'hospitality' I mean to refer to all human rights claims which are cross-border in scope. The tension between sovereignty and hospitality is all the more real for liberal democracies because they are based on the fragile but necessary negotiation of constitutional universalism and territorial sovereignty. Let me explore this by elaborating the paradox of democratic legitimacy.

The Paradox of Democratic Legitimacy

Ideally, democratic rule means that all members of a sovereign body are to be respected as bearers of human rights, and that the consociates of this sovereign freely associate with one another to establish a regime of self-governance under which each is to be considered both author of the laws and subject to them. This ideal of the original contract, as formulated by Jean-Jacques Rousseau and adopted by Kant, is a heuristically useful device for capturing the logic of modern democracies. Modern democracies, unlike their ancient counterparts, conceive of their citizens as rights-bearing consociates. The rights of the citizens rest on the "rights of man." "*Les droits de l'homme et du citoyen*" do not contradict one another; quite to the contrary, they are coimplicated. This is the idealized logic of the modern democratic revolutions following the American and French examples.

The democratic sovereign draws its legitimacy not merely from its act of constitution but, equally significantly, from the conformity of this act to universal principles of human rights that are in some sense said to precede and antedate the will of the sovereign and in accordance with which the sovereign undertakes to bind itself. "We, the people" refers to a particular human community, circumscribed in space and time, sharing a particular culture, history, and legacy; yet this people establishes itself as a democratic body by acting in the name of the "universal." The tension between universal human rights claims and particularistic cultural and national identities is constitutive of democratic legitimacy. Modern democracies act in the name of universal principles, which are then circumscribed within a particular civic community. This is the "Janus face of the modern nation," in the words of Juergen Habermas.[37]

Since Rousseau, however, we also know that the will of the democratic people may be legitimate but unjust, unanimous but unwise. "The general will" and "the will of all" may not overlap either in theory or in practice. Democratic rule and the claims of justice may contradict one another. The democratic precommitments expressed in the idealized allegiance to universal human rights—life, liberty, and property—need to be reactualized and renegotiated within actual polities as democratic intentions. Potentially, there is always a conflict between an interpretation of these rights claims that precede the declared formulations of the sovereign and the actual enactments of the democratic people, which could potentially violate such interpretations. We encounter this conflict in the history of political thought as the conflict between liberalism and democracy, and even as the conflict between constitutionalism and popular sovereignty. In each case, the logic of the conflict is the same: to assure that the democratic sovereign will uphold certain constraints on its will in virtue of its precommitment to certain formal and substantive interpretations of rights. Liberal and democratic theorists disagree with one another as to the proper balance of this mix: although strong liberals want to bind the sovereign will through precommitments to a list of human rights, strong democrats reject such a prepolitical understanding of rights and argue that they must be open to renegotiation and reinterpretation by the sovereign people—admittedly within certain limits.

Yet this paradox of democratic legitimacy has a corollary that has been little noted: every act of self-legislation is also an act of self-constitution. "We, the people" who agree to bind ourselves by these laws, are also defining ourselves as a "we" in the very act of self-legislation. It is not only the general laws of self-government that are articulated in this process; the community that binds itself by these laws defines itself by drawing boundaries as well, and these boundaries are territorial as well as civic. The will of the democratic sovereign can only extend over the territory that is under its jurisdiction; democracies require borders. Empires have frontiers, whereas democracies have borders. Democratic rule, unlike imperial dominion, is exercised in the name of some specific constituency and binds that constituency alone. Therefore, at the same time that the sovereign defines itself *territorially*, it also defines itself in *civic* terms. Those who are full members of the sovereign body are distinguished from those who "fall under its protection," but who do not enjoy "full membership rights." Women, slaves, and servants (many of who were women as well), propertyless white males, non-Christians, and nonwhite races historically were excluded from membership in the sovereign body and from the project of citizenship. They were, in Kant's famous words, "mere auxiliaries to the commonwealth."[38]

The boundaries of the civic community are of two kinds then: on the one hand, these boundaries define the status of those who enjoy second-class citizenship status within the polity but who can be considered members of the sovereign people in virtue of cultural, familial, and religious attachments. Women, as well as nonpropertied males before the extension of universal suffrage, fell under this category; the status of these groups is distinct from that of other residents who not only have second-class status but who also do not belong to the sovereign people in virtue of relevant identity-based criteria. Such was the status of African-American slaves until after the Civil War and the declaration in 1868 of the Fourteenth Amendment to the U.S. Constitution, which conferred U.S. citizenship on black people; such was also the status of American Indians who were granted tribal sovereignty. The status of those of Jewish faith in the original thirteen colonies of the United States can be described as one of transition from being "a mere auxiliary to the commonwealth" to being a full-fledged citizen.

In addition to these groups are those residents of the commonwealth who do not enjoy full citizenship rights either because they do not possess the requisite identity criteria through which the people defines itself, or because they belong to some other commonwealth, or because they choose to remain as outsiders. These are the "aliens" and "foreigners" amidst the democratic people. They are different from second-class citizens such as women and workers, as well as from slaves and tribal peoples. Their status is governed by mutual treaties among sovereign entities—as would be the case with official representatives of a state-power on the territory of the other; and if they are civilians, and live among citizens for economic, religious, or other cultural reasons, their rights and claims exist in that murky space defined by respect for human rights, on the one hand, and by international customary law, on the other. They are refugees from religious persecution, merchants and missionaries, migrants and adventurers, explorers and fortune-seekers.

I have circumscribed in general theoretical terms the paradox of democratic legitimacy. The paradox is that the republican sovereign should undertake to bind its will by a series of precommitments to a set of formal and substantive norms, usually referred to as "human rights." On closer examination, we see in fact that we are dealing with a dual paradoxical structure: on the one hand, between liberalism and democracy, that is between a promise to uphold human rights (however defined) and the will of democratic majorities; on the other hand, we face a paradox internal to democracies, namely, that democracies cannot choose the boundaries of their own membership democratically.[39]

Although this paradoxical structure can never be fully resolved, its impact can be mitigated through the renegotiation and reiteration of the dual commitments to human rights and sovereign self-determination. Popular sovereignty is not identical with territorial sovereignty, although the two are closely linked, both historically and normatively. Popular sovereignty means that all *full* members of the demos are entitled to have a voice in the articulation of the laws by which the demos governs itself. Democratic rule extends its jurisdiction to those who can view themselves as the authors of such rule. But there has never been a perfect overlap between the circle of those who stand under the law's authority and those recognized as full members of the demos. Every democratic demos has disenfranchised some, while recognizing only certain individuals as full citizens. Territorial sovereignty and democratic voice have never matched completely. Yet presence within a circumscribed territory, and in particular continuing residence within it, brings one under the authority of the sovereign—whether democratic or not. The new politics of cosmopolitan membership is about negotiating this complex relationship between rights of full membership, democratic voice and territorial residence. Although the demos, as the popular sovereign, must assert control over a specific territorial domain, it also can engage in reflex-ive acts of self-constitution, whereby the boundaries of the demos can be readjusted.

The evolution of cosmopolitan norms, from crimes against humanity to norms extending to refuge, asylum, and immigration have caught most liberal democracies within a network of obliga-tions to recognize certain rights claims. Although the asymmetry between the 'demos' and the 'populus,' the democratic people and the population as such, has not been overcome, norms of hospitality have gone far beyond what they were in Kant's understanding: the status of alienage is now protected by civil as well as international laws; the guest is no longer a guest but a resident alien, as we say in American parlance, or a "foreign co-citizen," as Europeans say. In a remarkable evolution of the norms of hospitality, within the European Union in particular, the rights of third-country nation-als are increasingly protected by the European Convention on Fundamental Rights and Freedoms, with the consequence that citi-zenship, which was once the privileged status entitling one to rights, has now been disaggregated into its constituent elements. Liberal democracies must learn to negotiate these paradoxes between the spread of cosmopolitan norms and the boundedness of democratic communities; that they can do so successfully is the topic, as well as the hope, of the second chapter.

Notes

1. *Hannah Arendt-Karl Jaspers Correspondence:1926–1969*, ed. Lotte Kohler and Hans Saner, trans. Robert and Rita Kimber (New York: Harcourt Brace Jovanovich, 1992), pp. 409–410. All future references in the text are to this edition and are referred to as "*Correspondence*."

2. In the Epilogue to *Eichmann in Jerusalem*, written several years later, Arendt no longer considers the analogy of Eichmann's crime to "piracy"

useful, and points out that "[The] pirate's exception to the territorial principle—which, in the absence of an international penal code, remains the only valid principle—is made not because he is the enemy of all, and hence can be judged by all, but because his crime is committed in the high seas, and the high seas are no man's land." Hannah Arendt, *Eichmann in Jerusalem: A Report on the Banality of Evil*, rev. and enl. ed. (New York: Penguin Books, [1963] 1994), p. 261. All future references in the text are to this edition and referred to as "*Eichmann 1963*."

3. Although technically the Charter of the International Military Tribunal (the Nuremberg tribunal) defined 'crimes against humanity' only with reference to crimes committed during international armed conflicts, after the Genocide Convention was adopted by the UN General Assembly on December 9, 1948, genocide also was included as a crime against humanity but left distinct due to its own jurisdictional status.

4. The use of force and in particular war have always been regulated, in the words of Clausewitz, "by imperceptible limitations hardly worth mentioning, known as international law and custom" (von Clausewitz, "On War," cited in Michael Howard, "*Temperamenta Belli:* Can War be Controlled?" in *Restraints on War*, Michael Howard, ed. [Oxford: Oxford University Press, 1979], p. 1.) From the Christian scholastic notion of "just war" to the "laws of war and peace" formulated by the moderns, there have always been some normative limitations on the conduct of war. Well aware of this tradition, the Nazi High Command attempted to present the Jews as "the national enemy" of the German people and claimed that the World Jewish Congress had declared war against the Nazis. The Nazis knew very well that the state-directed slaughter of innocent men, women, and children was against the law of "war crimes." But because of the specific nature of the racial genocide of the Jews, which had little to do with their imagined or real strategic place in Nazis war plans, a novel category—that of "crimes against humanity"—had to be fashioned so as to underline the particularly heinous aspect of murdering innocent children and civilians belonging to a people who had declared no hostility against Germany.

5. Arendt notes, with considerable irony, that Eichmann declared that he had lived his life according to Kantian moral precepts and the Kantian definition of duty. When one of the outraged Judges of the Israeli Court, Judge Raveh, questioned Eichmann, he defined the categorical imperative

as follows: "I meant by my remark about Kant that the principle of my will must always be such that it can become the principle of general laws" (as quoted by Arendt in *Eichmann* 1963, 136). Arendt further comments that in the "period of crimes legalized by the state," Eichmann had not just dismissed the formula of the categorical imperative, but he had distorted it to read "Act as if the principle of your actions were the same as that of the legislator or of the law of the land" (*Eichmann* 1963, 136). Eichmann conflated morality with positive law by claiming that his actions were moral because they were "legal."

An extreme version of this view is attributable to Carl Schmitt, who holds that "while the many 'monstrous atrocities' of the Hitler regime deserved to be solemnly condemned (though even they did not become classifiable under 'usual positive law') the concept of 'criminalization' should not be used in international law (it would break the citizen's duty of loyalty to his state)." Martti Koskenniemi, *The Gentle Civilizer of Nations: The Rise and Fall of International Law, 1870–1960* (Cambridge: Cambridge University Press, 2002), p. 418, n. 20. Koskemmieni cites Schmitt's *Das internationalrechtliche Verbrechen des Angriffskrieges und der Grundsatz, "Nullum crimen, nulla poena sine lege" (No crime, no punishment without law)* (Berlin: Duncker and Humboldt, 1994).

6. By "political existentialism" in this context I mean that, according to some commentators, Arendt saw political will and action as creating their own norms for judgment and evaluation, thus rejecting that they could be judged in accordance with extraneous standards, whether of morality, legality or aesthetics. I do not think that this interpretation of Arendt is correct yet it has been voiced powerfully by Martin Jay. See Martin Jay and Leon Botstein, "Hannah Arendt: Opposing Views," *Partisan Review* 45/3 (1978); reprinted as "The Political Existentialism of Hannah Arendt," in M. Jay, *Permanent Exiles* (New York: Columbia University Press, 1986), pp. 237–256, and George Kateb, *Hannah Arendt: Politics, Conscience, Evil* (Totowa, N.J.: Rowman and Allenheld, 1984) and "Political Action: its nature and advantages," in *The Cambridge Companion to Hannah Arendt*, ed. Dana Villa (Cambridge: Cambridge University Press, 2000), pp. 130–151. In this essay, Kateb explores "the authentically political" in Arendt's work in its relation to Max Weber and Carl Schmitt.

7. See Anne-Marie Slaughter's lucid statement: "International law today is undergoing profound changes that will make it far more effective

than it has been in the past. By definition international law is a body of rules that regulates relations among states, not individuals. Yet over the course of the 21st century, it will increasingly confer rights and responsibilities directly on individuals. The most obvious example of this shift can be seen in the explosive growth of international criminal law." In "Leading Through Law," *The Wilson Quarterly*. Special Section on "What Good Is International Law?" (Autumn 2003), pp. 42–43.

8. For the 'thin' view of globalization, see Thomas Friedman, *The Lexus and the Olive Tree: Understanding Globalization* (New York: Farrar, Straus Giroux, 1999); Michael Hardt and Antonio Negri, *Empire* (Cambridge, Mass.: Harvard University Press, 2000).

9. See Martha Nussbaum, "Patriotism and Cosmopolitanism," in *For Love of Country: Debating the Limits of Patriotism*, ed. Joshua Cohen (Boston, Mass.: Beacon Press, 1996), pp. 3–17; Jeremy Waldron, "Minority Cultures and the Cosmopolitical Alternative," in *The Rights of Minority Cultures*, ed. Will Kymlicka (Oxford: Oxford University Press, 1995), pp. 93–119; Jürgen Habermas, "Kant's Idea of Perpetual Peace, with the Benefit of Two Hundred Years' Hindsight," in *Perpetual Peace: Essays on Kant's Cosmopolitan Ideal*, ed. James Bohman and Matthias Lutz-Bachmann (Boston: MIT Press, 1997), pp. 113–155; James Bohman, "The Public Spheres of the World Citizen," in ibid., pp. 179–201; David Held, "Cosmopolitan Democracy and the Global Order: A New Agenda," in ibid., pp. 235–253; David Held, *Democracy and the Global Order: From the Modern State to Cosmopolitan Governance* (Cambridge: Polity Press, 1995).

10. For further elaboration, see Benhabib, *The Rights of Others: Aliens, Residents and Citizens* (Cambridge: Cambridge University Press, 2004), pp. 12–20.

11. Legal positivism is a complicated and rich tradition, with distinct lineages in Anglo-Saxon and Continental jurisprudence. Not all legal positivists would subscribe to the "command view of the law," defended by Hobbes and further developed by John Austin (1788–1859). This is best captured by Thomas Hobbes's phrase, "And Covenants, without the sword, are but Words . . . " [Hobbes, *Leviathan*, ed. and with an Introduction by C. B. McPherson (London: Penguin Books [1651] 1968), ch. xvii, p. 223]. For a comprehensive account of the status of international law, and of the underlying philosophical puzzles associated with it, see Marti Koskenniemi, *The Gentle Civilizer of Nations: The Rise and Fall of*

International Law 1870–1960 (Cambridge: Cambridge University Press, 2001), pp. 39–54.

For Arendt and Jaspers in the continental tradition, the relevant reference points would be Max Weber's and Hans Kelsen's rather than Austin's or Hobbes's views. See Hans Kelsen, *Pure Theory of Law* [*1934*], trans. Max Knight (Berkeley and Los Angeles: University of California Press, 1960).

Weber, as is well known, described the authority of the modern state and its bureaucracy as being based on the "legal-rational" paradigm and differentiated such a source of authority from other charismatic, substantive as well as democratic impositions of values on the legal system. See Max Weber, "The Types of Legitimate Domination," ch. III in *Economy and Society: An Outline of Interpretive Sociology*, ed. by Guenther Roth and Claus Wittich (Berkeley: University of California Press, 1978), pp. 212 ff. and note 12 below.

12. See Max Weber's statement: "'Equality before the law' and the demand for legal guarantees against arbitrariness demand a formal and rational 'objectivity' of administration, as opposed to the personally free discretion flowing from the 'grace' of the old patrimonial domination. If, however, an 'ethos'—not to speak of instincts—takes hold of the masses on some individual question, it postulates *substantive* justice oriented toward some concrete instance and person; and such an 'ethos' will unavoidably collide with the formalism and the rule-bound and cool 'matter-of-factness' of bureaucratic administration. For this reason, the ethos must emotionally reject what reason demands." "Bureaucracy," in *From Max Weber: Essays in Sociology*, H. H. Gerth and C. Wright Mills (New York: Oxford University Press, 1974 reprint), pp. 220–221.

13. See Hannah Arendt: ". . . the human condition is not the same as human nature . . . ," *The Human Condition* (Chicago: University of Chicago Press, 1958), p. 10.

14. See, for example, the objections of the American representative to the category of 'laws of humanity' during international negotiations after World War I: "As pointed out by the American Representatives on more than one occasion, war was and is by its very nature inhuman, but acts consistent with the laws and customs of war, although these acts are inhuman, are nevertheless not the object of punishment of this court. A judicial tribunal only deals with existing law and only administers existing law, leaving to another forum infractions of the moral law and contrary to the laws

and principles of humanity." U.S. Representatives on the Commission of Responsibilities, *Memorandum of Reservations to the Majority Report*, April 4, 1919, excerpted in Michael Marrus, *The Nuremberg War Crimes Trial 1945–46: A Documentary History* (New York: Bedford/St. Martin's, 1997), p. 10.

15. I have dealt more extensively with Kant's doctrine of cosmopolitanism in *The Rights of Others: Aliens, Citizens and Residents*, ch. 1.

16. I disagree with Jeremy Waldron's reading of Kant's theory in terms of anthropological assumptions concerning the fact that the earth is round, that therefore human beings must inevitably come into contact with one another, and the like. These anthropological observations correspond to that we might call, borrowing a term from Rawls, "the circumstances of cosmopolitan justice"; they neither serve as a philosophical foundation to it nor are they the most important innovation in it. See Jeremy Waldron, "What is Cosmopolitan?" *The Journal of Political Philosophy* 8, no. 2 (2000): 227–243, here p. 238. See Jeremy Waldron, "Cosmopolitan Norms" and my Reply in this volume.

17. The Articles are titled "The Civil Constitution of Every State should be Republican," "The Law of Nations shall be founded on a Federation of Free States," and "The Law of World Citizenship Shall be Limited to Conditions of Universal Hospitality." Much scholarship on this essay has focused on whether Kant meant to propose the establishment of a world federation of republics (*eine foederative Vereinigung*) or a league of sovereign nation-states (*Voelkerbund* or *Staatenbund*). I have used the following Kant editions: Immanuel Kant, "Zum Ewigen Frieden. Ein philosophischer Entwurf" [1795], in *Immanuel Kants Werke (Shriften von 1790–1796)*, ed. A. Buchenau, E. Cassirer and B. Kellermann (Berlin: Verlag Bruno Cassirer, 1923), pp. 425–474. Referred to in the text as "Kant [1795] 1923"; Immanuel Kant, "Perpetual Peace: A Philosophical Sketch" [1795], trans. H. B. Nisbet, in *Kant: Political Writings*, ed. Hans Reiss, 2nd and enl. ed. (Cambridge: Cambridge University Press, 1994), pp. 93–131. Referred to in the text as "Kant [1795] 1994."

18. David Held, "Law of States, Law of Peoples: Three Models of Sovereignty," *Legal Theory* 8 (2002): 1–44; here pp. 4ff.

19. Ibid., 4.

20. Michael Ignatieff, *Human Rights as Politics and Idolatry*, with Commentary by K. Anthony Appiah, David Hollinger, Thomas W. Laquer,

and Diane F. Orentlicher (Princeton, N.J.: Princeton University Press, 2001), p. 12.

21. See Hannah Arendt, *The Origins of Totalitarianism*, new ed. with added prefaces (New York: Harcourt Brace Jovanovich, repr.1979 [first ed. was published in 1951; new ed. published in 1966]), pp. 296–299.

22. Article 6 (c), Charter of the International Military Tribunal, as cited in James Friedman, "Arendt in Jerusalem, Jackson at Nuremberg: Presuppositions of the Nazi War Crimes Trials," *Israel Law Review* 28, no. 4 (1994): 601–625; here p. 614.

23. See Georg Cavallar, *The Rights of Strangers: Therories of International Hospitality, the Global Community and Political Justice since Vitoria* (Aldershot: Ashgate, 2002).

24. Richard Tuck, *The Rights of War and Peace: Political Thought and International Order from Grotius to Kant* (Cambridge: Cambridge University Press, 1999).

25. See Karl Jaspers, *The Origin and Goal of History*, trans. Michael Bullock (New Haven, Conn.: Yale University Press, 1953), pp. 193–213.

26. Such examples would include the UN treaty bodies under the International Covenant on Civil and Political Rights, the International Covenant on Economic, Social and Cultural Rights, the International Convention on the Elimination of All Forms of Racial Discrimination, the Convention on the Elimination of All Forms of Discrimination Against Women, the Convention Against Torture and other Cruel, Inhuman or Degrading Treatment or Punishment, and the Convention on the Rights of the Child. The establishment of the European Union has been accompanied by a Charter of Fundamental Rights. The European Convention for the Protection of Human Rights and Fundamental Freedoms, which encompasses states that are not EU members as well, permits the claims of citizens of adhering states to be heard by a European Court of Human Rights. Parallel developments can be seen on the American continent through the establishment of the Inter-American System for the Protection of Human Rights and the Inter-American Court of Human Rights. See Gerald Neuman, "Human Rights and Constitutional Rights: Harmony and Dissonance," *Stanford Law Review* 55, no. 5 (May 2003): 1863–1901. By 'soft law' is meant an international agreement that is not concluded as a treaty and therefore not covered by the Vienna Convention on the Law of Treaties. Such arrangements are adopted by states that do not want a

treaty-based relationship and do not want to be governed by treaty or customary law in the event of a breach of their obligations.

27. Carl Schmitt, *The Concept of the Political*, trans., intro., and notes by George Schwab (Chicago: University of Chicago Press, [1927] 1996).

28. "Human Rights and Constitutional Rights," p. 1875.

29. Charter of the International Military Tribunal, 1945, Art. 6 (c) as cited in Steven R. Ratner and Jason S. Abrams, *Accountability for Human Rights Atrocities in International Law: Beyond the Nuremberg Legacy* (New York: Clarendon Press: [1997] 2001 rev. and exp. ed.), pp.26–45; William A. Schabas, *An Introduction to the International Criminal Court* (Cambridge: Cambridge University Press, 2001), pp. 6–7.

30. Ratner and Abrams, *Accountability for Human Rights Atrocities*, pp. 35–36.

31. Ibid., pp. 80–110; Schabas, *Introduction to the International Criminal Court*, pp. 40–53.

32. Allen Buchanan, "From Nuremberg to Kosovo: The Morality of Illegal International Legal Reform," *Ethics* 111 (July 2001): 673–705.

33. Michael Doyle, "The New Interventionism," in *Global Justice*, ed. Thomas W. Pogge (Oxford and Mass.: Basil Blackwell, 2001), pp. 219–242.

34. Text available at: http://www.unhchr.ch/udhr/lang/eng.htm.

35. For the first position, see David Jacobson, *Rights Across Borders: Immigration and the Decline of Citizenship* (Baltimore and London: Johns Hopkins University Press, 1997), p. 5; for the second, Onora O'Neill, *Bounds of Justice* (Cambridge: Cambridge University Press, 2000), p. 180.

36. "Law of States, Law of Peoples," p. 1. In this article, Held develops cosmopolitanism into a "moral and political outlook," characterized by adherence to seven principles such as equal worth and dignity; active agency; personal responsibility and accountability; consent; reflexive deliberation; inclusiveness and subsidiarity; avoidance of serious harm and the amelioration of urgent need (p. 24). I am puzzled by this list and fear that with this move, cosmopolitanism is understood by Held as a "comprehensive doctrine" in Rawls's sense [see John Rawls, *Political Liberalism* (New York: Columbia University Press, 1993)]. A comprehensive doctrine entails not only a vision of justice but one of the good as well. I think that it is unnecessary and, from the standpoint of a Kantian cosmopolitan federalist understanding, incoherent, to make this move. What the elements of an "overlapping cosmopolitan consensus" may be is an

open question, but I disagree that one need commit oneself to a comprehensive account, such as the one Held provides. Furthermore, many of these principles are themselves aspects of a wide variety of moral theories, so it is unclear to me what is gained by incorporating them into cosmopolitanism.

37. Jürgen Habermas, "The European Nation-State: On the Past and Future of Sovereignty and Citizenship," in *The Inclusion of the Other: Studies in Political Theory,* ed. Ciaran Cronin and Pablo De Greiff (Cambridge, Mass.: MIT Press, 1998), pp. 105–129; here p. 115.

38. Immanuel Kant, "Die Metaphysik der Sitten in zwei Teilen" [1797], in *Immanuel Kants Werke,* p. 121; *The Metaphysics of Morals,* trans. and ed. Mary Gregor (Cambridge: Cambridge University Press, 1996), p. 140.

39. I thank Robert Post for noting the dual structure of this paradox.

Democratic Iterations

The Local, the National, and the Global

We are at a point in the political evolution of human communities when the unitary model of citizenship that bundled together residency on a single territory with subjection to a common bureaucratic administration representing a people perceived to be a more or less cohesive entity is at an end. We are facing today the 'disaggregation of citizenship.' These are institutional developments that unbundle the three constitutive dimensions of citizenship, namely, collective identity, the privileges of political membership, and the entitlements of social rights and benefits. More and more human beings, hailing from many parts of the world extending from North America to Europe to South Asia and Latin America, find themselves not sharing in the collective identity of their host countries while enjoying certain rights and benefits as guest workers or permanent residents. The entitlement to social rights, which T. H. Marshall had considered the pinnacle of citizenship, has been dissociated from shared collective identity and political membership.[1]

I begin by considering the disaggregation of citizenship; then, building on the promise of 'jurisgenerative politics,' I develop the concept of 'democratic iterations' as offering normative and institutional solutions to the paradoxes of democratic legitimacy.

Examining several cases from contemporary European debates concerning the rights of foreigners and immigrants, I illustrate processes of democratic iteration at work. Democratic iterations are complex ways of mediating the will- and opinion-formation of democratic majorities and cosmopolitan norms. In conclusion, I return to the ontological puzzles of cosmopolitan norms outlined in chapter 1.

Disaggregation of Citizenship within the European Union

Within the European Union, in which this disaggregation effect has proceeded most intensively,[2] the privileges of political membership now accrue to all citizens of member countries of the Union who may be residing in territories other than those of their nationality. It is no longer nationality of origin but EU citizenship that entitles one to these rights. Citizens of the EU can vote and stand for office in local elections in their host countries; they also can participate in elections to the European Parliament. If they are long-term residents in their respective foreign countries, on the whole they are also entitled to an equivalent package of social rights and benefits.

The condition of the EU's third-country nationals, whose countries of origin do not belong to the EU, is of course different. Although European Union citizenship makes it possible for all EU citizens to vote, run for, and hold office in local as well as Union-wide elections, this is not the case for third-country nationals. Their entitlement to political rights remains attached to their national and cultural origins. Yet in this respect as well changes are visible throughout the EU: in Denmark, Sweden, Finland, and Holland, third-country nationals can participate in local and regional elections; in Ireland these rights are granted at the local but not the regional level. In the United Kingdom, Commonwealth citizens can vote in national elections as well.

The most important conclusion to be drawn from these developments is that the entitlement to rights is no longer dependent on the status of citizenship; legal resident aliens have been incorporated into civil and social rights regimes, as well as being protected by supra- and subnational legislations. The condition of undocumented aliens, as well as of refugees and asylum seekers, however, remains in that murky domain between legality and illegality. Until their applications have been approved, refugees and asylums seekers are not entitled to choose freely their domicile or to accept employment. On the whole, refugees and those given asylum are entitled to certain forms of medical care; in some cases, their children can attend school. Undocumented migrants, by contrast, are cut off from rights and benefits and mostly live and work in clandestine conditions. The conflict between *sovereignty* and *hospitality* has weakened in intensity but it has by no means been eliminated. In fact, the EU is caught in contradictory currents that move it toward norms of cosmopolitan justice in the treatment of those who are within its boundaries, while leading it to act in accordance with outmoded Westphalian conceptions of unbridled sovereignty toward those who are on the outside. The negotiations regarding insider and outsider status have become tense and almost warlike.

The end of the unitary model of citizenship, therefore, does not mean that its hold on our political imagination or its normative force in guiding our institutions have grown obsolete. It does mean that we must be ready to imagine forms of political agency and subjectivity that anticipate new modalities of political citizenship. In the era of cosmopolitan norms, new forms of political agency have emerged that challenge the distinctions between citizens and long-term residents, insiders and outsiders. The spread of cosmopolitan norms, under whose aegis the disaggregation of citizenship proceeds, has led to contestations of the boundaries of the demos. Using the concepts of 'jurisgenerative politics' and 'democratic iterations,' I would first like to propose an analytical and normative grid for thinking about these transformations.

Democratic Iterations

'Iteration' is a term that was introduced into the philosophy of language through Jacques Derrida's work.[3] In the process of repeating a term or a concept, we never simply produce a replica of the original usage and its intended meaning: rather, every repetition is a form of variation. Every iteration transforms meaning, adds to it, enriches it in ever-so-subtle ways. In fact, there really is no "originary" source of meaning, or an "original" to which all subsequent forms must conform. It is obvious in the case of language that an act of original meaning-giving makes no sense, because, as Wittgenstein famously reminded us, to recognize an act of meaning-giving as precisely this act, we would need to possess language itself.[4] A patently circular notion!

Nevertheless, even if the concept of 'original meaning' makes no sense when applied to language as such, it may not be so ill-placed in conjunction with documents such as laws and other institutional norms. Thus, every act of iteration might be assumed to refer to an antecedent that is taken to be authoritative. The iteration and interpretation of norms, and of every aspect of the universe of value, however, is never merely an act of repetition. Every iteration involves making sense of an authoritative original in a new and different context. The antecedent thereby is reposited and resignified via subsequent usages and references. Meaning is enhanced and transformed; conversely, when the creative appropriation of that authoritative original ceases or stops making sense, then the original loses its authority on us as well. Iteration is the reappropriation of the "origin"; it is at the same time its dissolution as the original and its preservation through its continuous deployment.

Democratic iterations are linguistic, legal, cultural, and political repetitions-in-transformation, invocations that also are revocations. They not only change established understandings but also transform what passes as the valid or established view of an authoritative precedent.

Robert Cover and, following him, Frank Michelman have made these observations fruitful in the domain of legal interpretation. In "Nomos and Narrative," Robert Cover writes:

... there is a radical dichotomy between the social organization of law as power and the organization of law as meaning. This dichotomy, manifest in folk and underground cultures in even the most authoritarian societies, is particularly open to view in a liberal society that disclaims control over narrative. *The uncontrolled character of meaning exercises a destabilizing influence upon power. Precepts must "have meaning," but they necessarily borrow it from materials created by social activity that is not subject to the strictures of provenance that characterize what we call formal lawmaking.* Even when authoritative institutions try to create meaning for the precepts they articulate, they act, in that respect, in an unprivileged fashion.[5] (Emphasis added)

The disjunction between law as power and law as meaning can be rendered fruitful and creative in politics through "jurisgenerative processes." In such processes, a democratic people, which considers itself bound by certain guiding norms and principles, engages in iterative acts by reappropriating and reinterpreting these, thereby showing itself to be not only the *subject* but also the *author of the laws* (Michelman). Whereas natural right philosophies assume that the principles that undergird democratic politics are impervious to transformative acts of popular collective will, and whereas legal positivism identifies democratic legitimacy with the correctly generated legal norms of a sovereign legislature, jurisgenerative politics is à model that permits us to think of creative interventions that mediate between universal norms and the will of democratic majorities. The rights claims that frame democratic politics on the one hand must be viewed as transcending the specific enactments of democratic majorities under specific circumstances; on the other hand, such democratic majorities *reiterate* these principles and incorporate them into democratic will-formation processes through argument, contestation, revision, and rejection.

Because they are dependent on contingent processes of democratic will-formation, not all jurisgenerative politics yields positive results. In contrast to enacted legislation, the *validity of cosmopolitan norms* is not dependent on jurisgenerative and democratic iterations. This validity is based on independent normative grounds. Productive or creative jurisgenerative politics results in *the augmentation of the meaning of rights claims* and in *the growth of the political authorship by ordinary individuals*, who thereby make these rights their own by democratically deploying them.

Sterile, legalistic, or populistic jurisgenerative processes are conceivable. We may use Robert Cover's term "jurispathic" to refer to such processes.[6] In some cases, no normative learning may take place at all, but only a strategic bargaining among the parties may result; in other cases, the political process may simply run into the sandbanks of legalism or the majority of the demos may trample on the rights of the minority in the name of some totalizing discourse of fear and war. Jurisgenerative politics is not a politics of teleology or theodicy. Rather, it permits us to conceptualize those moments when a space emerges in the public sphere when principles and norms that undergird democratic will become permeable and fluid to new semantic contexts, which enable the augmentation of the meaning of rights.

In the following, I focus on two complex legal, political, and cultural phenomena through which democratic iterations have occurred and collective resignifications have emerged.[7] I begin with the so-called scarf affair, or "*l'affaire du foulard*," which preoccupied French public opinion and politics throughout the 1990s and still continues to do so. The banning of the wearing of the headscarf by Muslim girls in schools in the early 1990s pitted the right to freedom of conscience, to which all French citizens and residents alike are entitled, against the specific French understanding of the separation of church and state, known as the principle of *laïcité*. This affair led to an intense and unending debate about the meaning of French citizenship for an increasingly multicultural and multifaith society. The extension of a democratic schedule of rights to citizens and residents alike in a member country of the European Union, such as France, brings in its wake controversy about who precisely the subject of rights is. Can a Muslim woman be a good French citizen and also be true to herself? What exactly does it mean to be a "good" French citizen? Who defines the terms here?

On February 10, 2004, the French National Assembly voted by an overwhelming majority of 494 for and 36 against (with 31 abstentions) to ban the wearing of all religious symbols from public schools.

Although the new law applies to any ostentatiously displayed religious symbol such as Christian crosses and the "yarmulkes" of Orthodox Jewish students, as well as the headscarves worn by Muslim girls, its main target was Muslim religious attire. To understand the severity of this legislation, which drew criticism even from France's allies in the European Union, such as the British and the Dutch governments, it is important to reconstruct the history of the scarf affair.[8]

"L'Affaire du Foulard" (the Scarf Affair)

A consequence of transformations of citizenship is the long- and short-term coexistence of individuals and groups belonging to distinct and often quite contradictory cultures, mores and norms in the same public space.[9] If globalization brings with it the ever-rapid movement of peoples and goods, information and fashion, germs and news across state boundaries, one consequence of these trends is their multidirectionality. Globalization does not simply mean the spread of multinational, and usually American-, British-, or Japanese-run corporations, around the globe. Benjamin Barber's phrase "Jihad vs. McWorld" certainly captures a truth.[10] There is also the phenomenon of "reverse globalization," through which the peoples of the poorer regions of the world hailing from the Middle East, Africa, and South-East Asia flock to global cities, such as London and Paris, Toronto and Rome, Madrid and Amsterdam. These groups, a good number of whom originally came to Western countries as guest workers and immigrants, have seen their numbers multiply in the last decades through their children, born in migration, as well as through the entry of refugees and asylum seekers from other regions of the world. The most spectacular examples of multicultural conflict that have recently occupied public consciousness, such as the Salman Rushdie affair in Great Britain, the affair over the "foulard" (headscarf) in French schools, and scandals around the practice of female circumcision, have concerned new ethno-cultural groups, as they have sought to adapt their religious and cultural beliefs to the legal and cultural environment of secular, but mostly Protestant, Catholic, or Anglican, liberal democratic states.

"L'affaire du foulard"[11] originally began with a long and drawn-out set of public confrontations in France in 1989 with the expulsion from their school in Creil (Oise) of three scarf-wearing Muslim girls. Seven years later, the mass exclusion of twenty-three Muslim girls from their schools in November 1996 on the decision of the Conseil d'Etat took place.[12] Throughout the late 1990s and well into the first couple of years of the twenty-first century, confrontations between school authorities and young Muslim girls and women continued.

The affair, referred to as a "national drama"[13] or even a "national trauma,"[14] occurred in the wake of France's celebration of the second centennial of the French Revolution and seemed to question the foundations of the French educational system and its philosophical principle, laïcité. This concept is hard to translate with terms such as the "separation of church and state" or even "secularization": at its best, it can be understood as the public and manifest neutrality of the state toward all kinds of religious practices, institutionalized through a vigilant removal of sectarian religious symbols, signs, icons, and items of clothing from official public spheres. Yet within the French Republic the balance between respecting the individual's right to freedom of conscience and religion, on the one hand, and maintaining a public sphere devoid of all religious symbolisms, on the other, was so fragile that it only took the actions of a handful of teenagers to expose this fragility. The ensuing debate went far beyond the original dispute and touched on the self-understanding of French republicanism for the left as well as the right, on the meaning of social and sexual equality, and on liberalism versus republicanism versus multiculturalism in French life.

The affair began when on October 19, 1989, M. Ernest Chenière, headmaster of the college Gabriel-Havez of Creil, forbade three girls—Fatima, Leila, and Samira—to attend classes with their heads covered. The three had appeared in class that morning wearing their scarves, despite a compromise reached between their headmasters and their parents encouraging them to go unscarved. The three girls had apparently decided to wear the scarf once more on the advice of M. Daniel Youssouf Leclerq, the head of an organization called *Integrité* and the ex-president of the National Federation of Muslims in France (FNMF). Although hardly noted in the press, the fact that the girls had been in touch with M. Leclerq indicates that wearing the scarf was a conscious political gesture on their part, a complex act of identification and defiance. In doing so, Fatima, Leila, and Samira, on the one hand, claimed to exercise their freedom of religion as French citizens; on the other hand, they exhibited their Muslim and North African origins in a context that sought to envelop them within an egalitarian, secularist ideal of republican citizenship as students of the nation.

In the years to come, the girls and their followers and supporters forced what the French state wanted to view as a private symbol—an individual item of clothing—into the shared public sphere, thus challenging the boundaries between the public and the private. Ironically, they used the freedom given to them by French society and French political traditions, not the least of which is the availability of free and compulsory public education for all children on French soil, to transpose an aspect of their private identity into the public sphere. They problematized the school as well as the home: They no longer treated the school as a neutral space of French acculturation but brought their cultural and religious differences into open manifestation. They used the symbol of the home to gain entry into the public sphere by retaining the modesty required of them by Islam in covering their heads; yet, at the same time, they left the home to become public actors in a civil public space in which they defied the state. Those who saw in the girls' actions simply an indication of their oppression were just as blind to the symbolic meaning of their deeds as those who defended their rights simply on the basis of freedom of religion.

The French sociologists Gaspard and Khosrokhavar capture this set of complex symbolic negotiations as follows:

[The veil] mirrors in the eyes of the parents and the grandparents the illusions of continuity whereas it is a factor of discontinuity; it makes possible the transition to otherness (modernity), under the pretext of identity (tradition); it creates the sentiment of identity with the society of origin whereas its meaning is inscribed within the dynamic of relations with the receiving society.... It is the vehicle of the passage to modernity within a promiscuity which confounds traditional distinctions, of an access to the public sphere which was forbidden to traditional women as a space of action and the constitution of individual autonomy.[15]

The complexity of the social and cultural negotiations hidden behind the simple act of veiling elicited an equally ambiguous and complex decision by the French Conseil d'Etat. On November 4, 1989, the French minister of education, Lionel Jospin, took the matter to the Conseil d'Etat. The Conseil responded by citing France's adherence to constitutional and legislative texts and to international conventions, and invoked from the outset the necessity of doing justice to two principles: that the laïcité and neutrality of the state be retained in the rendering of public services, and that the liberty of conscience of the students be respected. All discrimination based on the religious convictions or beliefs of the students would be inadmissible. The Conseil then concluded that

... the wearing by students, in the schools, of signs whereby they believe to be manifesting their adherence to one religion is itself not incompatible with the principle of laïcité, since it constitutes the exercise of their liberty of expression and manifestation of their religious beliefs; but this liberty does not permit students to exhibit [d'arborer] signs of religious belonging which, by their nature, by the conditions under which they are worn individually or collectively, or by their ostentatious or combative [revindicatif] character, would constitute an act of pressure, provocation, proselytizing or propaganda, threatening to the dignity or liberty of the student or to the other members of the educational community, compromising their health or their security, disturbing the continuation of instructional activities or the educational role of the instructors, in short, [that] would disturb proper order in the establishment or the normal functioning of public service.[16]

This Solomonic judgment attempted to balance the principles of laïcité and freedom of religion and conscience. Yet, instead of articulating some clear guidelines, the Conseil left the proper interpretation of the meaning of wearing of these signs up to the judgment of the school authorities. Not the individual students' own beliefs about what a religious scarf, or for that matter a *yarmulke* (skull cap worn by observant Jews) meant to them but its interpretation by the school authorities, and whether or not such articles could be seen as signs of provocation, confrontation, or remonstration, became the decisive factors in curtailing the students' freedom of religion. It is not difficult to see why this judgment encouraged both sides to the conflict to pursue their goals further and led to further repression through the promulgation on September 10, 1994, of the Bayrou Guidelines, issued by Minister of Education François Bayrou. Lamenting the ambiguities of the judgment of the Conseil for conveying an impression of "weaknesses" vis-à-vis Islamicist movements, the minister declared that students had the right to wear discrete religious symbols, but that the veil was not among them.[17]

"L'affaire du foulard" eventually came to stand for all dilemmas of French national identity in the age of globalization and multiculturalism: how is it possible to retain French traditions of laïcité, republican equality, and democratic citizenship in view of France's integration into the European Union, on the one hand, and the pressures of multiculturalism generated through the presence of second- and third-generation immigrants from Muslim countries on French soil, on the other hand? Would the practices and institutions of French citizenship be flexible and generous enough to encompass multicultural differences within an ideal of republican equality? As European integration and multiculturalist pressures continue, France will have to discover new models of legal, pedagogical, social, and cultural institutions to deal with the dual imperatives of liberal democracies to preserve freedom of religious expression and the principles of secularism.[18]

We appear to have a paradoxical situation here in which the French state intervenes *to dictate* more autonomy and egalitarianism in the public sphere than the girls themselves wearing the headscarves seem to wish for. But what exactly is the meaning of the girls' actions? Is this an act of religious observance and subversion, or one of cultural defiance, or of adolescent acting out to gain attention and prominence? Are the girls acting out of fear, out of conviction, or out of narcissism? It is not hard to imagine that their actions may involve all these elements and motives. The girls' voices are not heard in this heated debate; although there was a genuine public discourse in the French public sphere and a soul searching on the questions of democracy and difference in a multicultural society, as the sociologists Gaspard and Khosrokhavar pointed out, until they carried out their interviews, the girls' own perspectives were hardly listened to. Had their voices been heard and listened to,[19] it would have become clear that the meaning of wearing the scarf itself was changing from being a religious act to one of cultural defiance and increasing politicization. Ironically, it was the very egalitarian norms of the French public educational system that brought these girls out of the patriarchal structures of the home and into the French public sphere, and gave them the confidence and the ability to *resignify the wearing of the scarf.* Instead of penalizing and criminalizing their activities, would it not have been more plausible to ask these girls to account for their actions at least to their school communities, and to encourage discourses among the youth about what it means to be a Muslim citizen in a laïc French Republic? Unfortunately, the voices of those whose interests were most vitally affected by the norms prohibiting the wearing of the scarf under certain conditions were silenced.

I am not suggesting that legal norms should originate through collective discursive processes and outside the framework of legal institutions: the legitimacy of the law is not at stake in this example; rather, it is the *democratic legitimacy* of a lawful, but in my view, unwise and unfair decision that is at stake. It would have been both more democratic and fairer if the meaning of their actions were not simply dictated to these girls by their school authorities, and if they were given more of a public say in the interpretation of their own actions. Would or should this have changed the Conseil d'Etat's decision? Maybe not, but the clause which permitted the prohibition of "ostentatiously" and "demonstratively" displayed religious symbols should have been reconsidered. There is sufficient evidence in the sociological literature that in many other parts of the world as well Muslim women are using the veil as well as the *chador* to cover up the paradoxes of their own emancipation from tradition.[20] To assume that their intentions were purely the religious defiance of the secular state constrains these women's own capacity to write the meaning of their own actions, and, ironically, reimprisons them within the walls of patriarchal meaning from which they are trying to escape.

Learning processes would have to take place on the part of the Muslim girls as well: whereas the larger French society would have to learn not to stigmatize and stereotype as "backward and oppressed creatures" all those who accept to wear what appears at first glance to be a religiously mandated piece of clothing, the girls themselves and their supporters, in the Muslim community and elsewhere, have to learn to give a justification of their actions with "good reasons in the public sphere." In claiming respect and equal treatment for their religious beliefs, they have to clarify how they intend to treat the beliefs of *others* from different religions, and how, in effect, they would institutionalize the separation of religion and the state within Islamic tradition.

Despite the harshness of the recent legislation banning the scarf by the French National Assembly, there are many efforts to integrate Islam into mainstream French society. On April 14, 2003, the *New York Times* reported the formation of an official Muslim Council to represent the five million Muslims of France. Among other issues, the Council will deal with the rights of Muslim women in the workplace. Thus, Karima Debza, an Algerian-born mother of three is reported as saying, "I cannot find work here because of my head scarf. . . . But my head scarf is part of me. I won't take it off. We have to educate the state about why the scarf is so important," and she added, "and why there should be no fear of it."[21]

What Debza is asking for is no less than a process of democratic iteration and cultural resignification. Although she is urging her French co-citizens to reconsider the strict doctrine of laicism, which precludes her from appearing in public places with a symbol that bears religious meaning, she herself is resignifying the wearing of the scarf in terms that some have called a "Protestantization" of Islam. The covering of one's head, which in Islam as well as Judaism is an aspect of women's modesty and also, more darkly, an aspect of the repression of female sexuality that is viewed as threatening, is now reinterpreted as a *private* act of faith and conscience rather than as a communal act of faith and belonging. In presenting the wearing of the scarf as an aspect of her identity and her self-understanding as a Muslim, Mrs. Debza is transforming these traditional connotations and is pleading for reciprocal recognition from others of her right to wear the scarf, as long as doing so does not infringe on the rights of others. "Because my wearing the scarf," Mrs. Debza is saying, "is so fundamental to who I am" (her own words are "it is a part of me"), "you should respect it as long as it does not infringe on your rights and liberties." The wearing of the scarf is resignified as expressing an act of conscience and moral freedom.

Her point can be summarized thus: the protection of the equal right to religious freedom of all citizens and residents of France (a right also upheld by the European Convention for the Protection of Human Rights and Fundamental Freedoms) should be considered more fundamental—in Ronald Dworkin's terms, should "trump"— the clause concerning the specific separation of religion and state that France practices, namely laicism. In this process, Debza states, "we have to educate the state not to fear us"—a marvelous thought coming from an immigrant Muslim woman vis-à-vis the daunting traditions of French republicanism!

The challenge posed to French traditions of laïcité cannot be under-estimated and, clearly, the Stasi report as well as the decision of the French National Assembly to ban the wearing of all religious symbols, except those that are very small and hardly visible publicly, signal the firm resolve of French authorities and legislators to keep public spaces 'laic' by emptying them of any sectarian symbols. But the clause of the separation of religion and state, while being a cornerstone of liberal democracies, also permits significant democratic variation. Thus, the United Kingdom has a Church of England, whereas Germany subsidizes the three officially recognized denominations—Protestant, Catholic, and Jewish—through an indirect "church tax" known as "*Kirchensteuer*." It would be no exaggeration to add that the First Amendment to the U.S. Constitution concerning the separation of church and state has been periodically contested and democratically reiterated since its ratification in 1791. Its significance is never frozen in time; rather, it is repeatedly the site of intense public battles. By contrast, emerging out of the historical experience of intense anticler-icalism and antagonism toward the institutions of the Catholic Church, the French republican tradition finds itself faced today with an unprecedented challenge: how to accommodate demands for religious diversity in the context of global trends toward increasingly multicul-tural and multifaith societies? Is the republican public sphere, cher-ished by French traditions, really defaced when individuals of different races, colors, and faiths want to function in this very public carrying the signs and symbols of their private faiths and identities? Should their self-presentation through their particular identities be viewed as a threat to French understandings of citizenship?

In an explicit acknowledgment of the "changing face of France," both in the literal and figurative senses, during August 2003, thirteen women, eight of them of North African Muslim origin, and the rest African immigrants or the children of immigrants, were chosen to represent "Marianne," the icon of the Revolution, painted in 1830 by Eugène Delacroix, bare-chested and storming the barricades. Continuing the contentious national dialogue about the separation of church and state, these women wore the ancient Phrygian cap, a symbol of the French Revolution, rather than the Islamic veil or other ethnic or national headdress.[22] Yet paradoxically, the political body that has decided to honor these women as a countersymbol to others like Mrs. Debza who insist on wearing the headscarf also has empowered them to challenge the overwhelmingly white, male, and middle-aged French Assembly, only 12 percent of whose members are women. One of the new Marianne's is quoted as saying: "These Mariannes have made visible something that has been the reality of the last twenty years. Look at the National Assembly. It's all white, rich, male and well educated. Now we have entered their space. We exist."[23]

Culture matters; cultural evaluations are deeply bound up with interpretations of our needs, our visions of the good life, and our dreams for the future. Because these evaluations run so deep, as citizens of liberal democratic polities, we have to learn to live with what Michael Walzer has called "liberalism and the art of separation."[24] We have to learn to live with the otherness of others whose ways of being may be deeply threatening to our own. How else can moral and political learning take place, except through such encounters in civil society? The law provides the framework within which the work of culture and politics go on. The laws, as the ancients knew, are the walls of the city, but the art and passions of politics unfold within those walls and very often politics leads to the breaking down of these barriers or at least to assuring their permeability.

There is a dialectic between constitutional essentials and the actual politics of political liberalism. Rights, and other principles of the liberal democratic state, need to be periodically challenged and rearticulated in the public sphere in order to retain and enrich their original meaning. It is only when new groups claim that they belong within the circles of addressees of a right from which they have been excluded in its initial articulation that we come to understand the fundamental limitedness of every rights claim within a constitutional tradition as well as its context-transcending validity. The democratic dialogue, and also the legal hermeneutic one, are enhanced through the repositioning and rearticulation of rights in the public spheres of liberal democracies. The law sometimes can guide this process, in that legal reform may run ahead of popular consciousness and may raise popular consciousness to the level of the constitution; the law also may lag behind popular consciousness and may need to be prodded along to adjust itself to it. In a vibrant liberal multicultural democracy, cultural-political conflict and learning through conflict should not be stifled through legal maneuvers. The democratic citizens themselves have to learn the art of separation by testing the limits of their over-lapping consensus.

Although the intervention of French authorities to ban the wearing of the veil in the schools at first seemed like the attempt of a progres-sive state bureaucracy to modernize the "backward-looking" customs of a group, this intervention cascaded into a series of democratic itera-tions. These ranged from the intense debate among the French public about the meaning of wearing the scarf, to the self-defense of the girls involved and the rearticulation of the meaning of their actions, to the encouragement of other immigrant women to wear their headscarves into the workplace, and finally to the very public act of resignifying the face of "Marianne," via having immigrant women from Arab coun-tries as well as Africa represent her.

I do not want to underestimate, however, the extent of public dissat-isfaction with and significant xenophobic resentment toward France's Muslim population. Democratic iterations can lead to processes of public self-reflection as well as generating public defensiveness. The mobilization of many right-wing parties throughout Europe is inten-sifying: in France, the Netherlands, the United Kingdom, Denmark, Germany, Austria, and elsewhere, we see well that the status of Europe's migrants, and particularly of its Muslim population, remains an incendiary issue. Nevertheless, it is clear that all future struggles with respect to the rights of Muslim and other immigrants will be fought within the framework created by the universalistic principles of Europe's commitment to human rights, on the one hand, and the exigencies of democratic self-determination, on the other.[25]

Who Can Become a German Citizen? Redefining the Nation

On October 31, 1990, the German Constitutional Court ruled against a law passed by the provincial assembly of Schleswig-Holstein on February 21, 1989, which changed the qualifications for participating in local municipal (*Bezirk*) and district-wide (*Kreis*) elections.[26] According to Schleswig-Holstein's election laws in effect since May 31, 1985, all those who were defined as German in accordance with Article 116 of the Basic Law, who had completed the age of eighteen and who had resided in the electoral district for at least three months were eligible to vote. The law of February 21, 1989, proposed to amend this as follows: all foreigners residing in Schleswig-Holstein for at least five years, who possessed a valid permit of residency or who were in no need of one, and who were citizens of Denmark, Ireland, the Netherlands, Norway, Sweden, and Switzerland, would be able to vote in local and district-wide elections. The choice of these six countries was made on the grounds of reciprocity. Because these countries permitted their foreign residents to vote in local and in some cases regional elections, the German provincial legislators saw it appropriate to reciprocate.

The claim that the new election law was unconstitutional was brought by 224 members of the German Parliament, all of them members of the conservative CDU/CSU (Christian Democratic and Christian Social Union) party; it was supported by the Federal Government of Germany. The Court justified its decision with the argument that the proposed change of the electoral law contradicted "the principle of democracy," as laid out in Articles 20 and 28 of Germany's Basic Law, and according to which "All state-power [*Staatsgewalt*] proceeds from the people."[27]

The people [*das Volk*], which the Basic Law of the Federal Republic of Germany recognizes to be the bearer of the authority [*Gewalt*] from which issues the constitution, as well as the people which is the subject of the legitimation and creation of the state, is the German people. Foreigners do not belong to it. Membership in the community of the state [*Staatsverband*] is defined through the right of citizenship. . . . Citizenship in the state [*Staatsangehorigkeit*] constitutes a fundamentally indissoluble personal right between the citizen and the state. The vision [or image—Bild] of the people of the state [*Staatsvolkes*], which underlies this right of belonging to the state, is the political community of fate [*die politische Schicksalsgemeinschaft*], to which individual citizens are bound. Their solidarity with and their embeddedness in [*Verstrickung*] the fate of their home country, which they cannot escape [*sich entrinnen koennen*], are also the justification for restricting the vote to citizens of the state. They must bear the consequences of their decisions. By contrast, foreigners, regardless of however long they may have resided in the territory of the state, can always return to their homeland.[28]

This resounding statement by the Constitutional Court can be divided into three components: first, a disquisition on the meaning of *popular sovereignty* (all power proceeds from the people); second, a *procedural* definition of how we are to understand *membership* in the state; third, a philosophical explication of the nature of the bond between the state and the individual, based on the vision of a "*political community of fate.*" The Court argued that according to the principle of popular sovereignty, there needed to be a "congruence" between the concept of the people and the main guidelines for voting rights at all levels of state power—namely, federal, provincial, district, and communal. Different conceptions of popular sovereignty could not be employed at different levels of the state. Permitting long-term resident foreigners to vote would imply that popular sovereignty would be defined in different fashion at the district-wide and communal levels than at the provincial and federal levels. In an almost direct repudiation of the Habermasian discursive democracy principle, the Court declared that Article 20 of Germany's Basic Law does not imply that "the decisions of state organs must be legitimized through those whose interests are affected [*Betroffenen*] in each case; rather their authority must proceed from the people as a group bound to each other as a unity [*das Volk als eine zur Einheit verbundene Gruppe von Menschen*]."[29]

In its brief before the Constitutional Court, the provincial parliament of Schleswig-Holstein challenged the Court's understanding and argued that neither the principle of democracy nor that of the people excludes the rights of foreigners to participate in elections: "The model underlying the Basic Law is the construction of a democracy of human beings, and not that of the collective of the nation. This basic principle does not permit a distinction in the long-run between the people of the state [*Staatsvolk*] and an association of subservients [*Untertanenverband*]."[30]

The German Constitutional Court eventually resolved this controversy by upholding a unitary and functionally undifferentiated concept of popular sovereignty, but it did concede that the sovereign people, through its representatives, could change the definition of citizenship. Procedurally, "the people" simply means all those who have the requisite state membership. If one is a citizen, one has the right to vote; if not, not. "So the Basic Law . . . leaves it up to the legislator to determine more precisely the rules for the acquisition and loss of citizenship and thereby also the criteria of belonging to the people. The law of citizenship is thus the site at which the legislator can do justice to the transformations in the composition of the population of the Federal Republic of Germany." This can be accomplished by expediting the acquisition of citizenship by all those foreigners who are long-term permanent residents of Germany.[31]

The Court here explicitly addresses what I have called 'the paradox of democratic legitimacy' in the preceding chapter, namely, that those whose rights to inclusion or exclusion from the demos are being decided on will not themselves be the ones to decide on these rules. The democratic demos can change its self-definition by altering the criteria for admission to citizenship. The Court still holds on to the classical model of citizenship according to which democratic participation rights and nationality are strictly bundled together in a community of fate, but by signaling the procedural legitimacy of changing Germany's naturalization laws, the Court also acknowledges the power of the democratic sovereign to alter its self-definition such as to accommodate the changing composition of the population. The line separating citizens and foreigners can be renegotiated by the citizens themselves.

Yet the procedural democratic openness signaled by the Court stands in great contrast to a conception of the democratic people also adumbrated by the Court that views the people as "a political community of fate," held together by bonds of solidarity in which individuals are embedded (*verstrickt*). Here the democratic people is viewed as an *ethnos*, as a community bound together by the power of shared fate, memories, solidarity, and belonging. Such a community does not permit free entry and exit. Perhaps marriage with members of such a community may produce some integration over generations; but, by and large, membership in an ethnos—in a community of memory, fate, and belonging—is something into which one is born, although as an adult one may renounce this heritage, exit it, or wish to alter it. To what extent should one view liberal democratic polities as *ethnoi* communities? Despite its emphatic evocation of the nation as "a community of fate," the Court also emphasizes that the democratic legislator has the prerogative to transform the meaning of citizenship and the rules of democratic belonging. Such a transformation of citizenship may be necessary to do justice to the changed nature of the population. The demos and the ethnos do not simply overlap.

Written in 1990, in retrospect this decision of the German Constitutional Court appears as a swan song to a vanishing ideology of nationhood.[32] In 1993, the Treaty of Maastricht, or The Treaty on the European Union, established European citizenship, which granted voting rights and rights to run for office for all members of the fifteen signatory states residing in the territory of other member countries. Of the six countries to whose citizens Schleswig-Holstein wanted to grant reciprocal voting rights—Denmark, Ireland, the Netherlands, Norway, Sweden, and Switzerland—only Norway and

Switzerland remained nonbeneficiaries of the Maastricht Treaty because they were not EU members.

In the years following, an intense process of democratic iteration unfolded in the now-unified Germany, during which the German Constitutional Court's challenge to the democratic legislator of aligning the definition of citizenship with the composition of the population was taken up, rearticulated, and reappropriated. The city-state of Hamburg, in its parallel plea to alter its local election laws, stated this very clearly. "The Federal Republic of Germany has in fact become in the last decades a country of immigration. Those who are affected by the law which is being attacked here are thus not strangers but cohabitants [Inlaender], who only lack German citizenship. This is especially the case for those foreigners of the second and third generation born in Germany."[33] The demos is not an ethnos, and those living in our midst and who do not belong to the ethnos are not strangers either; they are rather "cohabitants," or as later political expressions would have it, "our co-citizens of foreign origin" [ausländische Mitbuerger].

Even these terms, which may sound odd to ears not accustomed to any distinctions besides those of citizens, residents and nonresidents, suggest the transformations of German public consciousness in the 1990s. This intense and soul-searching public debate finally led to an acknowledgment of the fact as well as the desirability of immigration. The need to naturalize second- and third-generation children of immigrants was recognized and a new German citizenship law was passed in January 2000. Ten years after the German Constitutional Court turned down the election law reforms of Schleswig-Holstein and the city-state of Hamburg on the grounds that resident foreigners were not citizens, and were thus ineligible to vote, Germany's membership in the European Union led to the disaggregation of citizenship rights. Resident members of EU states can vote in local as well as EU-wide elections; furthermore, Germany now accepts that it is a country of immigration; immigrant children become German citizens according to jus soli and keep dual nationality until the age of twenty-four, at which point they must choose either German citizenship or that of their country of birth. Furthermore, long-term residents who are third-country nationals can naturalize if they wish to do so.

Democratic Iterations and the Dialectic of Rights and Identities

With the cases of the scarf affair and German voting laws, I have sought to elucidate processes of democratic iteration that attest to a dialectic of rights and identities. In such processes, both the identities involved and the very meaning of rights claims are reappropriated, resignified, and imbued with new and different meaning. Political agents, caught in such public battles, very often enter the fray with a present understanding of who they are and what they stand for; but the process itself frequently alters these self-understandings. Thus, in the scarf affair in France, we witness the increasing courage, maybe even militancy, of a group of women considered usually to be 'docile subjects,' in Michel Foucault's sense.[34] Traditional Muslim girls and women are not supposed to appear in the public sphere at all; ironically, precisely the realities of Western democracies with their more liberal and tolerant visions of women's role permits these girls and women to be educated in public schools, to enter the labor force, and, in the case of Fereshda Ludin,[35] to even become a German teacher with the status of a civil servant. They are transformed from being 'docile bodies' into 'public selves.' Although they struggle at first to retain their *traditional and given identities,* as women they also become empowered in ways they may not have anticipated. They learn to *talk back to the state.* My prediction is that it is a matter of time before these women, who are learning to talk back to the state, also will engage and contest the very meaning of the Islamic traditions that they are now fighting to uphold. Eventually, these public battles will initiate private gender struggles about the status of women's rights within the Muslim tradition.[36]

These cases show that outsiders are not only at the borders of the polity but also within it. In fact, the very binarism between nationals and foreigners, citizens and migrants is sociologically inadequate and the reality is much more fluid, as many citizens are of migrant origin, and many nationals themselves are foreign-born. The practices of immigration and multiculturalism in contemporary democracies flow into one another.[37] Although the scarf affair both in France and Germany challenges the vision of the "homogeneity" of the people, the German Constitutional Court's decisions show that there may often be an incongruity between those who have the formal privilege of democratic citizenship (the demos) and others who are members of the population but who do not formally belong to the demos. In this case, the challenge posed by the German Court to the democratic legislature of adjusting the formal definition of German citizenship, such as to reflect the changing realities of the population, was taken up and the citizenship law was reformed. The democratic people can reconstitute itself through such acts of democratic iteration so as to enable the extension of democratic voice. Aliens can become residents, and residents can become citizens. Democracies require porous borders.

The constitution of "we, the people" is a far more fluid, contentious, contested and dynamic process than either Rawlsian liberals or decline-of-citizenship theorists would have us believe. The Rawlsian vision of peoples as self-enclosed moral universes is not only empirically but also normatively flawed.[38] This vision cannot do justice to the dual identity of the people as an *ethnos*, as a community of shared fate, memories, and moral sympathies, on the one hand, and as a *demos*, as a democratically enfranchised totality of all citizens, who may or may not belong to the same ethnos, on the other. All liberal democracies that are modern nation-states exhibit these two dimensions. The politics of peoplehood consists in their negotiation. The presence of so many migrants from Algeria, Tunisia, and Morocco, as well as from central Africa, testifies to France's imperial past and conquests, just as the presence of so many *Gastarbeiter* in Germany is a reflection of the economic realities of

Germany since World War II. Some would even argue that without their presence, the post–World War II German miracle would not have been conceivable.[39] Peoplehood is dynamic and not a static reality. A demos can alter its own understanding of citizenship, which in turn will alter the ethnos, understood as a shared community of fate.[40]

Decline-of-citizenship theorists, such as Michael Walzer and David Jacobson,[41] are just as wrong as Rawlsian liberals, in conflating the ethnos and the demos. They privilege the right of sovereign national communities to determine the rules of membership according to their cultural self-understanding and in accordance with desires to preserve cultural majorities. Human rights assume secondary importance in influencing the will of democracies. [42] The presence of others who do not share the dominant culture's memories and morals poses a challenge to the democratic legislatures to rearticulate the meaning of democratic universalism. Far from leading to the disintegration of the culture of democracy, such challenges reveal the depth and the breadth of the culture of democracy. Only polities with strong democracies are capable of such universalist rearticulation through which they refashion the meaning of their own peoplehood. Will French political traditions be less strong if they are now carried forth and reappropriated by Algerian women or women from the Côte d'Ivoire? Will German history be less confusing and puzzling if it is taught by an Afghani-German woman, as in the Fereshda Ludin case? Rather than the decline of citizenship, I see in these instances the reconfiguration of citizenship through democratic iterations.

Cosmopolitan Rights and Republican Self-Determination

I began with a puzzle, the first articulations of which I attributed to Hannah Arendt and Karl Jaspers. After the capture of Eichmann by

Israeli agents in 1960, Arendt and Jaspers initiated a series of reflections on the status of international law and norms of cosmopolitan justice. I summarized their queries in terms of three questions: What is the ontological status of cosmopolitan norms in a postmetaphysical universe (1)? What is the authority of norms that are not backed by a sovereign with the power of enforcement (2)? How can we reconcile cosmopolitan norms with the fact of a divided mankind (3)? I promised that I would begin by answering the last question first and then proceed to the others.

Ad. 3: My answer to the question as to how to reconcile cosmopolitanism with the unique legal, historical, and cultural traditions and memories of a people is that we must respect, encourage, and initiate multiple processes of democratic iteration. Not all such processes are instances of jurisgenerative politics. Jurisgenerative politics, at their best, are cases of legal and political contestation in which the meaning of rights and other fundamental principles are reposited, resignified, and reappropriated by new and excluded groups, or by the citizenry in the face of new and unprecedented hermeneutic challenges and meaning constellations. I have tried to illustrate such cases of "rights at work," in instances in which cosmopolitan norms that apply to the rights of residents or immigrant foreigners are rearticulated by constituted democratic legislatures. The French scarf affair and the German Constitutional Court's decision concerning the voting rights of resident foreigners are cases in which democratic majorities contested and redeployed cosmopolitan norms.

As we see in the French scarf affair, processes of democratic iteration do not invariably and necessarily result in political outcomes that we may want to endorse, whereas in the case of the German citizenship debate this has resulted in a liberalization of naturalization and immigration policies and in the enlargement of the boundaries of the demos. By contrast, with the passing of legislation banning the wearing of all religious symbols in the schools, the French state has intensified the confrontation with its observant populations, Jewish and Muslim alike. It is clear that future battles around this issue will take place inside and outside France. Along with the debate that is unfolding in the new Europe about the separation of church and state within the EU Constitution, France's strict understanding of laicism, deplored even by its closest neighbors, will itself be challenged at the highest levels of jurisgenerative politics. This is the peculiarity of cosmopolitan justice: precisely because France is a signatory to the European Convention for the Protection of Human Rights and Fundamental Freedoms as well as to the European Charter of Human Rights, even the actions and decisions of its National Assembly, are not immune to future juridical challenges.

Such controversies reenact in practice the theoretical dilemma of discursive scope: universalist norms are mediated with the self-understanding of local communities. The availability of cosmopolitan norms, however, increases the threshold of justification to which formerly exclusionary practices are now submitted. Exclusions take place, but the threshold for justifying them is now higher. This higher threshold also heralds an increase in democratic reflexivity. It becomes increasingly more difficult to justify practices of exclusion by democratic legislatures simply because they express the will of the people; such decisions are now subject not only to constitutional checks and balances in domestic law but in the international arena as well.

The French courts and politicians find it necessary to ban the wearing of religious symbols on the basis of grounds that can be generalized for all: it is the future well-being and integrity of French society, as a society of *all* its citizens, which is appealed to. Reflexive grounds appeal to reasons that would be valid for all. This means that such grounds can themselves be recursively questioned for failing to live up to the threshold set in their own very articulation.

Ad. 2: To Arendt's and Jaspers's second question as to the authority of cosmopolitan norms, my answer is: *the power of democratic forces within global civil society*. Of course, the global human rights regime by now has its agencies of negotiation, articulation, observation, and monitoring. In addition to processes of naming, shaming, and sanctions that can be imposed on sovereign nations in the event of egregious human rights violations, the use of power by the international community, as authorized by the UN Security Council and the General Assembly, remains an option. We are in a transitional period in the configuration of the world political community, when the doctrine of humanitarian interventions has pierced the shield of state sovereignty in problematic ways: on the one hand, that genocide in any country or region of the world triggers a generalized moral and legal obligation on the part of the world community to intervene is a fulfillment of cosmopolitan norms; on the other hand, this doctrine can be used inconsistently—why Bosnia alone? Why not Rwanda and Darfur as well?—and hypocritically—was the Iraq war of 2003 really a case of humanitarian intervention? We may need to envisage a transition from the 'soft power' of global civil society to the *constitutionalization of international law.*

Ad. 1: I come then to the final question: what is the ontological status of cosmopolitan norms in a postmetaphysical universe? Briefly, such norms and principles are morally constructive: they create a universe of meaning, values, and social relations that had not existed before by changing the normative constituents and evaluative principles of the world of "objective spirit," to use Hegelian language. They found a new order—a *novo ordo saeclorum.* They are thus subject to all the paradoxes of revolutionary beginnings. Their legitimacy cannot be justified through appeal to antecedents or to consequents: it is the fact that there was no precedent for them that makes them unprecedented; equally, we can only know their consequences once they have been adopted and enacted. The act that 'crimes against humanity' has come to name and to interdict was itself unprecedented in human history, that is, the mass murder of a human group on account of their race through an organized state power with all the legal and technological means at its disposal. Certainly, massacres, group murders, and tribal atrocities were known and practiced throughout human history. The full mobilization of state power, with all the means of a scientific-technological civilization at its disposal, in order to extinguish a human group on account of their claimed racial characteristics, was wholly novel. Once we name 'genocide' as the supreme crime against humanity, we move in a new normative universe. I would even dare say that we move into a universe which now contains a new moral fact—"Thou shalt not commit genocide and perpetrate crimes against humanity." I do not mean by this that the murder of innocent children, women, and civilians was never before considered a crime. That would be absurd. The taking of innocent life is one of the deepest taboos of many of the world's moral and religious systems. It is precisely because we as humankind have learned from the memories of genocide, extending from the African slave trade to the Holocaust of the European Jews, that we can name it as the supreme crime. Cosmopolitan norms, of which 'crimes against humanity' is the most significant, create such new moral facts by opening novel spaces for signification, meaning, and rearticulation in human relations.

Let us turn to Hannah Arendt once more. Although she was skeptical that international criminal law would ever be codified and properly reinforced, Arendt in fact praised and commended the judges who sought to extend existing categories of international law to the criminal domain. She wrote

... that the unprecedented, once it has appeared, may become a precedent for the future, that all trials touching upon 'crimes against humanity' must be judged according to a standard that is today still an 'ideal.' If genocide is an actual possibility of the future, then no people on earth ... can feel reasonably sure of its continued existence without the help and the protection of international law. Success or failure in dealing with the hitherto unprecedented can lie only in the extent to which this dealing may serve as a valid precedent on the road to international penal law.... In consequence of this as yet unfinished nature of international law, it has become the task of ordinary trial judges to render justice without the help of, or beyond the limitation set upon them through, positive, posited laws. (*Eichmann* 1963, 273–74)

However fragile their future may be, cosmopolitan norms have evolved beyond the point anticipated and then problematized by Hannah Arendt. An International Criminal Court exists, although the oldest democracy in the world, the United States, has refused to sign the Rome Treaty legitimizing it. The spread of cosmopolitan norms, from interdictions of war crimes, crimes against humanity and genocide to the increasing regulations of cross-border movements through the Geneva Conventions and other accords, has yielded a new political condition: the local, the national and the global are all imbricated in one another. Future democratic iterations will make their interconnections and interdependence deeper and wider. Rather than seeing this situation as undermining democratic sovereignty, we can view it as promising the emergence of new political configurations and new forms of agency, inspired by the interdependence—never frictionless but ever promising—of the local, the national, and the global.

Notes

1. T. H. Marshall, *Citizenship and Social Class and Other Essays* (London: Cambridge University Press, 1950). See also my essay, "Transformations of Citizenship: The Case of Contemporary Europe," *Government and Opposition: An International Journal of Comparative Politics* 37, no. 4 (2002): 439–465. I do not subscribe to the teleologism implicit in Marshall's catalogue of rights and have criticized his blind spots in *The Rights of Others. Aliens, Residents and Citizens*, pp. 171–173.

2. See Seyla Benhabib, *The Claims of Culture: Equality and Diversity in the Global Era* (Princeton, N.J.: Princeton University Press, 2002), chap. 6; and Benhabib, *The Rights of Others: Aliens, Citizens and Residents. The John Seeley Memorial Lectures* (Cambridge: Cambridge University Press, 2004), chap. 4.

3. Jacques Derrida, "Signature, Event, Context" [1971], in *Limited Inc.* (Evanston, Ill.: Northwestern University Press, 1988), pp. 90 ff. I am indebted to the insights of Judith Butler and Bonnie Honig in highlighting the significance of iterative practices for democratic politics. See Judith Butler, *Excitable Speech: Politics of the Performative* (New York and London: Routledge, 1997); Bonnie Honig, *Democracy and the Foreigner* (Princeton,

N.J.: Princeton University Press, 2001), and Honig, "Declarations of Independence: Arendt and Derrida on the Problem of Founding a Republic," *American Political Science Review* 85, no. 1 (March 1991): 97–113.

4. Ludwig Wittgenstein, *Philosophical Investigations*, trans. G. E. M. Anscombe (Oxford: Blackwell, 1953).

5. Robert M. Cover, "*Nomos* and Narrative," *Harvard Law Review* 97, no. 1 (1983): 4–68. Here page 18; Frank Michelman, "Law's Republic," *Yale Law Journal* 97, no. 8 (July 1988): 1493–1537.

6. Robert Cover, "Nomos and Narrative," 40–44; 53–60.

7. A more extensive discussion has appeared in Benhabib, *The Rights of Others*, chap. 5.

8. The first version of this chapter was written before I had a chance to examine in detail the report of the committee headed by Bernard Stasi submitted to the French President Jacques Chirac and preceding the French national vote. My reading of this report has convinced me that I was too optimistic in my interpretation of some of these developments. See "Rapport au President de la République," Commission de Réflexion sur l'Application du Principe du Laïcité dans la République; December 11, 2003. Available at: http://www.ladocumentationfrancaise.fr/brp/notices/034000725.shtml.

9. Parts of this discussion have previously appeared in Benhabib, *The Claims of Culture*, pp. 94–100.

10. Benjamin Barber, *Jihad vs. McWorld* (New York: Times Books, 1995).

11. A note of terminological clarification first: the practice of veiling among Muslim women is a complex institution that exhibits great variety across many Muslim countries. The terms *chador, hijab, niqab,* and *foulard* refer to distinct items of clothing that are worn by Muslim women coming from different Muslim communities: for example, the *chador* is essentially Iranian and refers to the long black robe and headscarf worn in a rectangular manner around the face; the *niqab* is a veil that covers the eyes and the mouth and only leaves the nose exposed; it may or may not be worn in conjunction with the *chador*. Most Muslim women from Turkey are likely to wear either long overcoats and a *foulard* (a headscarf) or a *carsaf* (a black garment that most resembles the *chador*). These items of clothing have a symbolic function within the Muslim community itself: women coming from different countries signal to one another their ethnic and

national origins through their clothing, as well as signifying their distance from or proximity to tradition in doing so. The brighter the colors of their overcoats and scarves—bright blue, green, beige, lilac as opposed to brown, gray, navy, and, of course, black-and the more fashionable their cuts and material by Western standards, all the greater is the distance from Islamic orthodoxy of the women who wear them. Seen from the outside, however, this complex semiotic of dress codes gets reduced to one or two items of clothing that then assume the function of crucial symbols in the complex negotiation among Muslim religious and cultural identities and Western cultures.

12. My discussion of these incidents relies primarily on two sources: *Le Foulard et la République*, by Francoise Gaspard and Farhad Khosrokhavar (Paris: Decouverte, 1995), and an excellent seminar paper by Marianne Brun-Rovet, "A Perspective on the Multiculturalism Debate: 'L'Affaire Foulard' and Laïcité in France, 1989–1999" (on file with the author). See also the more recent publication, *Alma et Lila Levy: Des Filles comme les Autres: Au-delà du Foulard*, interviews by Veronique Giraud and Yves Sintomer (Paris: La Decouverte, 2004).

13. Gaspard and Khosrokhavar, *Le Foulard et la République*, p. 11.

14. Brun-Rovet, "Perspective on the Multiculturalism Debate," p. 2.

15. Gaspard and Khosrokhavar, *Le Foulard et la République*, pp. 44–45 (my translation).

16. Ruling of the Conseil d'Etat, November 27, 1989.

17. *Le Monde*, September 12, 1994, 10. In the Report of the Stasi Commission (see note 8 above) even the terms of the objects of clothing change their meaning: it is no longer "the foulard" which is at issue—a scarf or bandanna worn around the head—but, rather, "la voile" (the veil), a transparent gauze, which would cover not only the hair but possibly the eyes, the nose, and the mouth and which is worn primarily by girls and women from Saudi Arabia and Kuwait, and hardly by French Muslims, who hail primarily from Algeria, Tunis, Morocco, and Turkey. This rhetorical shift signals a hardening of the fronts.

18. For an assessment of the intensity of the debate and the polarization caused by it, see "Derrière la Voile," *Le Monde Diplomatique* no. 599 (February 2004), pp. 6–9. Among the organizations opposing the legislation to ban the wearing of the headscarf in public schools were the League for Human Rights, the Movement against Racism and for Friendship

Among Peoples (MRAP), as well as the United Syndical Federation (FSU) and the Federation of Parents Councils (FCPE).

19. A recent publication tries precisely to let the girls speak for themselves. See *Alma et Lila Levy*, interviews by Giraud and Sintomer, cited in note 12 above.

20. Nilufer Gole, *The Forbidden Modern: Civilization and Veiling* (Ann Arbor: University of Michigan Press, 1996).

21. Elaine Sciolino, "French Islam Wins Officially Recognized Voice," *New York Times*, April 14, 2003, sec. A, p. 4.

22. Elaine Sciolino, "Paris Journal; Back to Barricades: Liberty, Equality, Sisterhood," *New York Times*, August 1, 2003, sec. A, p. 4.

23. Ibid.

24. Michael Walzer, "Liberalism and the Art of Separation," *Political Theory* 12 (August 1984): 315–330.

25. In recent years, the German public and the courts have dealt with a challenge quite akin to the scarf affair in France. An elementary school teacher in Baden-Wuerttemberg, Fereshda Ludin, of Afghani origin and German citizenship, insisted on being able to teach her classes with her head covered. The school authorities refused to permit her to do so. The case ascended all the way to the German Constitutional Court (BVerfG) and on September 30, 2003, the Court decided as follows. Wearing a headscarf, in the context presented to the Court, expresses that the claimant belongs to the "Muslim community of faith" (*die islamische Religionsgemeinschaft*). The court concluded that to describe such behavior as lack of qualification (*Eignungsmangel*) for the position of a teacher in elementary and middle schools clashed with the right of the claimant to equal access to all public offices in accordance with Article 33, Paragraph 2 of the Basic Law (*Grundgesetz*), and also clashed with her right to freedom of conscience, as protected by Article 4, Paragraphs 1 and 2 of the Basic Law, without, however, providing the required and sufficient lawful reasons for doing so (BVerfG, 2BvR, 1436/02, IVB 1 and 2; my translation). While acknowledging the fundamental rights of Fereshda Ludin, the Court nevertheless ruled against the claimant and transferred the final say on the matter to the democratic legislatures. "The responsible provincial legislature is nevertheless free to create the legal basis [to refuse to permit her to teach with her head covered—SB], by determining anew within the framework set by the constitution, the extent of religious articles to be permitted in the schools.

In this process, the provincial legislature must take into consideration the freedom of conscience of the teacher as well as of the students involved, and also the right to educate their children on the part of parents as well as the obligation of the state to retain neutrality in matters of world-view and religion" (BVerfG, 2BvR, 1436/02, 6). This case is discussed more extensively in Benhabib, *The Rights of Others*, chap. 5.

26. BVerfG, vol. 83, II, Nr. 3, p. 37; in the following, all translations from the German are mine. A similar change in its election laws was undertaken by the free state of Hamburg in order to enable those of its foreign residents of at least eight years to participate in the election of local municipal assemblies (*Bezirkversammlungen*). Because Hamburg is not a federal province (*Land*) but a free city-state, with its own constitution, some of the technical aspects of this decision are not parallel to those in the case of Schleswig-Holstein. I chose to focus on the latter case alone. It is nonetheless important to note that the Federal Government, which had opposed Schleswig-Holstein's electoral reforms, supported those of Hamburg. See BVerfG 83, 60, II, Nr. 4, pp. 60–81.

27. BVerfG 83, 37, Nr. 3, p. 39.

28. BVerfG 83, 37, Nr. 3, pp. 39–40.

29. BVerfG 83, 37, II, Nr. 3, p. 51.

30. BVerfG, 83, 37, II, p. 42.

31. BVerfG 83, 37, II, Nr. 3, 52.

32. I do not mean to suggest that nationalist ideologies and sentiments vanished from the unified Germany. However, unlike in many of Germany's neighboring countries such as France and the Netherlands, they did lose considerable institutional traction throughout the 1990s. New citizenship laws were passed by parliamentary majorities of Social Democrats, Greens, and Christian Democrats; but the price for the liberalization of citizenship was paid in terms of further restrictions on Germany's rather generous asylum laws. So these transitions were not without cost. Nationalism reappeared on the German scene first when one million signatures were collected in a referendum in Hesse against permitting dual citizenship of immigrant children who are now entitled to this only until they are twenty-four; the second instance was the recent Iraq war and deep fear and dislike of the U.S. Administration under George Bush; and the third case was the surprisingly racialized debate about Turkey's admission to membership talks in the EU (Fall 2004).

33. B VerfG 83, 60, II, Nr. 4, 68. The brief filed by the city-state of Hamburg differed from that filed by Schleswig-Holstein in that Hamburg did not restrict the granting of the vote to foreigners to the six states mentioned on the basis of reciprocity alone but wanted to give the vote to participate in the election of local municipal assemblies (*Bezirksversammlungen*) to all those who had been legal residents for eight years. This decision would have included large numbers of Turkish guest workers and their children.

34. Michel Foucault, *Discipline and Punish: The Birth of the Prison*, trans. Alan Sheridan (New York: Pantheon Books, 1997).

35. See note 25 for a discussion of her case.

36. The French "scarf affair" is being followed very closely in Turkey, a secular, multiparty democracy, the majority of whose population is Muslim. Throughout the 1980s and 1990s, Turkey confronted its own version of the scarf affair as the Islamist parties increased their power in Parliament and unprecedented numbers of Turkish Islamist women began attending the universities. From the standpoint of Turkish state authorities, the scarf is seen as a violation of the principle of *"laiklik"* (laïcité) articulated by Atatuerk, the founder of the Republic. The Turkish Constitutional Court decided in 1989 against the use of scarves as well as turbans in universities. Students and the Islamist organizations representing them appealed to Article 24 of the Turkish Constitution, which guarantees freedom of religious expression, and to Article 10, which prohibits discrimination due to religious belief and differences in language, ethnicity and gender. Their appeals were rejected. Although officially the wearing of the "turban" (a form of headscarf worn by observant Muslim women) is banned, many faculty members as well as administrators tolerate it when they can. See Benhabib, *The Claims of Culture*, p. 203.

37. See Benhabib, *The Claims of Culture*, pp. 165–177.

38. John Rawls, *The Law of Peoples* (Cambridge, Mass.: Harvard University Press, 1999), pp. 23–35, and my critique in Benhabib, *The Rights of Others*, chap. 3.

39. James F. Hollifield, *Immigrants, Markets, and States: The Political Economy of Postwar Europe* (Cambridge, Mass., and London: Harvard University Press, 1992).

40. I thank Robert Post for this formulation and clarification.

41. Michael Walzer, *Spheres of Justice: A Defense of Pluralism and*

Equality (New York: Basic Books, 1983); David Jacobson, *Rights Across Borders: Immigration and the Decline of Citizenship* (Baltimore and London: The Johns Hopkins University Press, 1997).

42. I have discussed Michael Walzer's position on immigration and citizenship in Seyla Benhabib, *The Claims of Culture: Equality and Diversity in the Global Era* (Princeton, N.J.: Princeton University Press, 2002), pp. 172–175, and decline of citizenship theories more generally in *The Rights of Others*, pp. 114–124.

Comments

Cosmopolitan Norms

Jeremy Waldron

"Cosmopolitanism," Professor Benhabib rightly observes, "has become one of the keywords of our times" (17). But "cosmopolitan" has a number of different meanings.[1] For some, it is about the love of mankind, or about duties owed to every person in the world, without national or ethnic differentiation. For others, the word "cosmopolitan" connotes the fluidity and the evanescence of culture; it celebrates the compromising or evaporation of the boundaries between cultures conceived as distinct entities; and it anticipates a world of fractured and mingled identities.[2] For still others—and this is the theme that Benhabib explores—cosmopolitanism is about order and norms, not just culture and moral sentiment. It envisages a world order, and (in some views) a world government or world polity. According to the cosmopolitan, there are already many norms in the world which operate at a cosmopolitan level, including (for example) the principles that define human rights and crimes against humanity, the laws that govern refuge, asylum, travel, and migration, and the dense thicket of rules that sustain our life together, a life shared by people and peoples, not just in any particular society but generally on the face of the earth.

The last category I mentioned—the dense thicket of rules that sustain our life together—includes some of the most mundane things imaginable: postal and telephone conventions, airline safety and navigation standards, the law of international trade, the practices that define the convertibility of currencies, transnational banking arrangements, weights and measures, time zones, international quarantine arrangements, and so on. Philosophers and political theorists are not much interested in these unexciting issues. We have nothing to say on currency rates, bills of sale, the maintenance of sea lanes, cell-phone standards, or the Warsaw Convention governing the liability of airlines to their passengers. We don't like commerce (because we are largely ignorant of it), and we would prefer not to have to write about it. However, it will be part of my argument that in asking questions about the emergence and the status of cosmopolitan norms, we have to focus at least as much on these quotidian norms as on the high profile issues, such as *l'affaire du foulard*, on which every political theorist, it seems, has something exciting to say.

So: there is this array of cosmopolitan norms that structure our lives together. Considered not just with reference to particular societies but as lives lived *in the world*, the interaction of people and peoples on the face of the earth is not an anarchy. Although there is no world state, these interactions exhibit a certain order, which we may call a cosmopolitan order. That there is such an order is clear enough. People may disagree about how old it is and whether to call it "a *new* world order." They may disagree about how extensive it is. But its existence, as something more than a dream or an aspiration is undeniable. The problem is how to characterize it. In her lectures, Professor Benhabib posed two sets of questions about this cosmopolitan order, one about substance and one about provenance:

First, as to substance: what is the content of this order? What are these existing or emerging cosmopolitan norms? What issues do they address? What do they require? What obligations or values do they impose upon us? As with any norms, we need to know the answers to this set of questions in order to expound, evaluate, and (if necessary) criticize, oppose, and change this cosmopolitan order.

Second, as to provenance: where does the ordering come from? Is it imposed (like legislation) and if so, by whose authority? How is it sustained, upheld, and enforced? This second cluster of questions can be asked in several different ways. Professor Benhabib asks: what are the ontological foundations of cosmopolitan norms? In a "postmetaphysical" world, we cannot simply equate them with the law of nature's God. They are something less than *lex naturae*, but they seem to have a solidity that goes beyond mere sentiment or idealism. So what, fundamentally, *are* they? A less elevated way of asking the same question draws on some old distinctions between law and morality and between legal and social norms. Does this cosmopolitan order represent anything more than the widespread acceptance and influence of certain moral ideals of humanity, decency, honesty and fair dealing? Or is it even less than that? Among businessmen, we know, and among property-owners, merchants, traders, and those in all walks of life, social norms often exist which complement or even outstrip existing orders of positive law.[3] Is that what cosmopolitan norms are, just emergent social norms that have little to do with law (as that concept is ordinarily understood)?

Both sets of questions are important, not least because they challenge us to think about how cosmopolitan norms relate to the legal orders of particular societies and nation-states. We think we know how *national* law works:[4] there are legislatures and lawbooks, courts and constitutions, sheriffs and police officers, primary and secondary rules. It may turn out of course that asking questions about cosmopolitan norms undermines or complicates the understanding of municipal law that we think we possess; in recent years, jurists have shown an increasing awareness of the way in which municipal legal orders sustain themselves with reference to a legal heritage and to connections among jurists that go well beyond national boundaries.[5] But still we approach cosmopolitan norms with some settled jurisprudential assumptions, which we developed in the first instance with regard to municipal law.

So far as the first question is concerned—what is the content of the cosmopolitan order?—we often find an interesting duplication of subject-matter as between cosmopolitan norms and rules of municipal law. Particularly when we move away from international law in the strict sense (that is the law regulating relations among states), we find not so much a division of labor as juridical redundancy. International human rights conventions are mirrored in national constitutions and Bills of Rights;[6] and international commercial and transportation conventions often require member states to enact legislation according to their terms (i.e., according to the terms of the international conventions). And yet, we still think—some of us—that the world is richer for having this second layer of norms, even if it does not add much to the accumulated positive law of particular countries, even if all it does is coordinate and help standardize the provisions of the various systems of municipal law.

I shouldn't exaggerate. Sometimes there is disparity between cosmopolitan norms and municipal law, and the content of the cosmopolitan norms may challenge some of the substantive assumptions embodied in municipal law and national politics. But then that leads us to the second question. Are cosmopolitan norms anything more than ideas about how municipal law should be changed? If that is what cosmopolitan norms are — just critical ideals for municipal law—then it might be an analytic mistake to treat them as laws in their own right.

The second question—Where do these norms come from?—invites us to consider how cosmopolitan norms differ in their modes of existence, validity, application, and enforcement from the norms of municipal law. Municipal law applies within national boundaries, but we think of cosmopolitan norms as open and unbounded in their application. Municipal law is enacted by representatives of the national community to whose members it applies, but there is no similar doctrine of democratic enactment for cosmopolitan norms. Professor Benhabib rightly focuses our attention on these two issues, figuring that each of them makes some difference, and that their combination establishes a crucial difference, as between the cosmopolitan order and a municipal legal order. In the case of municipal law, the members of a national community are able to identify law as a concrete artifact of their politics; they can answer the ontological question in that way. More than that, they can view the law imposed on them by the state as in some sense "theirs." They can say to one another, "This not just law that applies to us; this law is *ours*—we own it—even when we do not altogether agree with the rights and obligations that it establishes." In Rousseau's political theory, a set of norms that can be conceived in this way is a different sort of order from one that is merely imposed. Indeed, Rousseau reserves the word "law" for just this kind or ordering.[7] But none of this seems to work for the cosmopolitan order. Although it applies to the people of the world, it does not seem to be "ownable" by them in the same sort of way: there is not the same Rousseauian correlation between its provenance in their politics, the generality of its formal application to them, and the spirit of solidarity that informs it. Maybe it is a little strong to say, as Professor Benhabib says, that there is a dilemma at the heart of the idea of cosmopolitan law. I shall return to this at the end of my comments. But certainly there is a massive and so far quite mysterious difference between thinking of cosmopolitan norms as law and thinking in legal terms about the norms of an ordinary municipal system. Until we have something more to say about the former, the idea of a cosmopolitan order remains unanalyzed. I think Professor Benhabib's notion of "democratic iteration" contributes a substantial amount of what is needed here, to resolve this obscurity. But in what follows I shall pursue that idea in a slightly different way from the way in which she pursues it.

The first set of questions was about the substance or the content of cosmopolitan norms. What are these norms about? The outset of her lectures indicates that Professor Benhabib has a particular interest in norms defining "crimes against humanity" and by extension human rights norms and what she called "cosmopolitan norms of justice" (13, 15). What distinguishes these from the more familiar rules of international law is that cosmopolitan norms offer rights and protections to, and impose obligations on, human individuals as such not just states. But Benhabib is clear that she does not want to "reduce cosmopolitan norms to a thin version of the human rights to life, liberty, equality, and property, which are supposed to accompany the spread of free markets and trading practices" (16). So, what more do they involve? One of the ways Professor Benhabib wants to enrich our understanding of the content of cosmopolitan norms is by reference to Immanuel Kant's essay *Towards Perpetual Peace*, and also to the discussion of "cosmopolitan right" at the end of the first part, the *Rechtslehre*, of Kant's book *The Metaphysics of Morals*.[8] She makes considerable use of Kant and I shall follow her in regarding this discussion as one of our most useful philosophical resources in regard to these difficult questions.

The center of Kant's account of "cosmopolitan right" is what he calls "hospitality," which he describes in *Perpetual Peace* as "the right of a foreigner not to be treated with hostility because he has arrived on the land of another"[9] Kant says that the principle requiring hospitality more or less exhausts the content of cosmopolitan right—"Cosmopolitan right shall be limited to conditions of universal hospitality"[10]—and accordingly Professor Benhabib thinks it important to dwell on the meaning of "hospitality." Now, on the face of it, the principle of hospitality seems quite a limited principle. It seems to concern the particular duty that each of us (or each people, or each nation) owes to strangers who fetch up on our shores. It is not hard to read into Kant's principle a right of sojourn, even a right of refuge or asylum, but it may be a bit of a stretch to say, as Professor Benhabib says, toward the end of her first lecture: "In a Kantian vein, by 'hospitality' I mean to refer to all human rights claims which are cross-border in scope" (31). Let me be clear: I am not complaining about the mere fact that a lot is being read into this principle. For one thing, we are talking about a principle not just a rule. Hospitality is a deep or background idea that informs an array of norms rather than a single norm in its own right.[11] For another thing, as Benhabib says, Kant warns us that he is using the term "hospitality" in an unusual sense (21–22). And anyway, there would be no point in reading these antiquated Prussian tracts if we did not stretch and distort them a bit to throw some light on our current concerns.[12]

But I wonder whether Professor Benhabib pursues her interpretation in the right direction. She talks sometimes as though hospitality were about our relation to one another "as potential participants in a world republic" (22) or at least in the world federation that Kant envisaged. I agree with her that Kant's speculations about a world federation as a means of ensuring peace are extremely interesting, and it is true that he uses the term "cosmopolitan constitution" to refer to the legal order that he has in mind for such a federation.[13] At the same time, we have to take note of the fact that Kant sharply differentiated between "cosmopolitan right" and what he called "the right of nations," and that he associated the principle of hospitality with the former not the latter.[14] The right of nations—what we would call the jurisprudence of international law—is the appropriate location for Kant's speculations about world federation and a "cosmopolitan constitution," but it may distort our understanding of cosmopolitan hospitality if we associate it too closely with those ideas.

Here is one way in which this distortion may occur. In his writings about the right of nations, Kant argued for a voluntary federation of nations rather than a world state. He conjectured that a world state might be "more dangerous to freedom" than the warfare it was supposed to supersede, "by leading to the most fearful despotism (as has indeed happened more than once with states which have grown too large)."[15] As I read this argument, it is entirely pragmatic concerning the likely effects on freedom of various juridical arrangements. But Professor Benhabib presents it as a more positive affirmation of the nation-state principle. She writes: "Kant argued that cosmopolitan citizens still needed their individual republics to be citizens at all" (24). Now, obviously there is room for disagreement here about Kant's view of the inherent importance of state-sized political communities. It becomes a problem, however, when Benhabib associates the view about the inherent importance of national political communities (which she attributes to Kant) with the principle of hospitality that dominates his account of cosmopolitan right. I don't think hospitality is about states or political communities at all, whether at the level of a world republic or an individual republic. It is about relations between people and peoples, and it needs to be read in that determinedly *non*-state-centered way in order to capture the distinctive contribution it is supposed to make to Kant's practical philosophy.

Professor Benhabib and I agree in offering expansive readings of hospitality. But where I would stretch our understanding of Kant's concept is in the direction of travel, contact, and commerce—the myriad processes by which humans, at all levels of *social* organization, all over the world, come into direct or indirect contact with one another. Each person, Kant says, has the right to visit—a right to present oneself before others, with a view to interaction. He associated this right with two duties—on the one side, a duty not to treat another with hostility simply because he shows up with a view to contact or commerce, and, on the other side, a duty not to treat one's visit or commercial approach as an occasion for oppression or exploitation. Kant's discussion of hospitality comes in the midst of his ferocious criticism of European colonial exploitation in America, Africa, and the Indies—places, he says, where Europeans "drink wrongfulness like water."[16] Like us, he is critical of this violence, injustice, and exploitation; unlike us, however, he does not see it just as a question of the behavior of states or national conquerors but also of traders and merchants and settlers who come to distant lands on their own initiative. His general point is that, in spite of the manifest potential for injustice and in spite of the actual experience of injustice, there is nothing inherently unjust or inappropriate about individually initiated contacts among peoples. People must be permitted to come into contact with one another, if only "by virtue of the right of possession in common of the earth's surface on which, as a sphere, they cannot disperse infinitely but must finally put up with being near one another."[17] They must be permitted to offer to deal with one other. A mere approach is not to be regarded as an offense. The commercial and other interactions that the technology of transportation makes possible must be regarded as inevitable and desirable. They are not unjust *per se*; they are unjust only if they lead to independently defined forms of violence or exploitation. Kant's position on hospitality is that we are to keep this in mind as the underlying premise of all our thinking about contacts between peoples.

We can take this perhaps one step further and see Kant's account of hospitality as foreshadowing an early version of some recent criticisms of the politics of cultural identity.[18] I think the duty of hospitality and the corresponding right to visit evince a certain attitude toward culture, which is like the second form of cosmopolitanism that I emphasized at the very beginning of these comments. Kant's position is that the mere fact that a group of explorers and merchants from one culture want to make contact with members of another culture is not to be regarded in itself as an affront. No doubt such contacts will compromise the identity and purity of one or both of the cultures (that is what contact—commerce, intercourse, conversation—*is*). But that in itself is not to be regarded as a ground for hostility or concern. To put it the other way round: if Kant *had* regarded the identity and integrity of particular cultures as something to be preserved, something whose preservation was basic to this area of right, then he would have presented the background right to visit in quite a different light, hedging it round with all sorts of restrictions, not only of consent, but of something like cultural quarantine. Certainly the sanguine way in which he envisages cosmopolitan community—something which comes very close to being the *telos* of cosmopolitan right—is quite incompatible with either the purity or the integrity that is sometimes associated with cultural identity politics.

It is not just a matter of Kant's happening to prefer communication among peoples to the idea of each culture in its splendid isolation. The circumstantial propositions about the peoples of the world living side-by-side within a determinate and spherical space, of their being unable to flee decisively from contact with one another, not to mention the prevalence of human curiosity and the urge to discover—all this means that even for a proponent of cultural integrity, isolation would be a lost cause. Both the outward circumstances of the world and the natural temper of mankind militate against cultural isolation, apart from the most exceptional circumstances.[19] True, Kantian principles *need* not bow to the pressure of factual inevitability in this way; and Kant does not rule out the possibility of a society sealing itself off against outside contact at least for a time. (He cites the cases of contemporary China and Japan.)[20] It's more that the inevitability of contact makes it more or less impossible to regard purity, homogeneity, and splendid isolation as the normal condition of culture, and thus it makes it impossible to regard the contamination of a culture by external contact as the sort of affront that in itself could reasonably be thought to be at stake in a stance of principled opposition to intercultural commerce.

In some of my other work on Kant's political philosophy, I have connected this reading of hospitality with what I call his "principle of proximity"—the idea that states are to be formed among those who are "unavoidably side-by-side" and likely to enter into conflict with one another in the absence of juridical arrangements, whether they share anything in the way of national, ethnic, or cultural affinity or not.[21] I worry that Benhabib's reading of Kant's preference for national community detracts from the distinctiveness of this emphatically non-nationalist view, just as her state-centered account of hospitality detracts from the distinctiveness of his conception of cosmopolitan order. But there is not time to explore that further issue in these comments. It is enough for the moment to express some concern lest this imputed solicitude for national community be treated as a moral obstacle to the dealings between cultures that are the very essence of Kantian cosmopolitan right.

The second set of question is about the status or ontology of cosmopolitan norms. What sort of norms are they? Where do they come from? Are they law? If so, how are they imposed and by whose authority? The way these questions are answered is also affected, I think, by the difference between my approach to Kantian hospitality and the more state-centered approach taken by Professor Benhabib.

Benhabib wants to rule out two possible answers to the question of the ontological status of cosmopolitan norms—that they are natural law and that they are positive law. I agree that it would be a mistake to think of cosmopolitan norms as natural law in the sense that modern moral philosophers claim to study natural law. That sense often involves little more than the moralizing of an individual over some issue of right or justice accompanied by a meta-ethical claim to objectivity so far as that moralizing is concerned. But cosmopolitan norms reflect a worldly reality that involves more than just individuals' moralizing in an objectivist mood.

So are they positive law? Well, the rights and duties that Professor Benhabib calls cosmopolitan norms of justice are not positive law at least in the following sense: they don't exist as sovereign commands upheld with steel or institutionalized in a Hobbesian way. And it would probably not be a good thing if they were; as we have already seen, Benhabib associates herself with Kant's observation that a world government, enforcing its own positive law on a global scale in a Hobbesian way, might lead "to the most fearful despotism."[22]

But legal positivism is a variegated class of jurisprudential doctrine and—as Benhabib points out (20), we must be careful not to oversimplify it by associating it too closely with Hobbesian command. Positive law can involve commands and sanctions. But it also can involve customs and practices. These can be immemorial customs—such as the burial laws for which Antigone risked death and of which she said: "Their life is not of to-day or yesterday, but from all time, and no man knows when they were first put forth."[23] Or they can be more recently evolving customs, growing out of but also constituting a social order and a shared and mutually expressible sense that our interactions with others are governed by norms, even when there is no one to enforce them. (H. L. A. Hart's famous contribution to jurisprudence was to see that the social existence of certain custom-like practices—which he called "secondary rules"—had to be considered the basis of a jurisprudence of enacted rules, rather than the other way round, as in the theory of Hobbes and Austin.)[24]

Earlier, I mentioned commercial interaction as a paradigm of interaction under the auspices of Kantian hospitality. Commercial interaction—in this and other contexts—also provides a good example of the emergence of custom. We often forget how much the practices of trade precede the growth of commercial law. People trade first—between distinct societies—and they develop the customary norms of trading *in their commerce*. That customary law grows up along the trade routes. It is not imposed by anyone, and it is not enforced by any apparatus except merchants keeping track of one another. Indeed, what we call the commercial law of particular countries is to a great extent a development out of this phenomenon—the *lex mercatoria*[25]—rather than the other way round. Even though it is not commanded by any state or power-center, or backed up with sanctions, the *lex mercatoria* has nevertheless a positive rather than a purely notional or moralistic existence. My aim here is not to glorify commerce as a source of norms. The emphasis on commerce in this section and the last is primarily intended as a way of redirecting attention away from the high-profile issues where cosmopolitanism seems at its most spectacular and challenging, to the dense detail of ordinary life in which people routinely act and interact as though their dealings were conducted within some sort of ordered framework, even though that framework has not been imposed or laid down by anything like a state. The example of commerce, in other words, is appealed to as a prototype of how the mundane growth of repeated contact between different humans and different human groups can lay the foundation for the emergence of cosmopolitan norms, in a way that does not necessarily presuppose a formal juridical apparatus.

Kant, I said, was a ferocious critic of some contemporary colonial and mercantile practices.[26] But when he reflected on his criticisms he observed that these were not just subjective or philosophical reactions. His convictions in the realm of cosmopolitan right were not just some bright normative idea that he thought up (in the way that a modern political philosopher in New England might *think up* a new theory of justice). His work on cosmopolitan right has a positive, expository dimension that addresses norms that he recognizes would exist in the world whatever some philosopher in Konigsberg thinks. This is what Kant is referring to when he says things such as the following: "[T]he (narrower or wider) community of the nations of the earth has now gone so far that a violation of right on one party of the earth is felt in all."[27] The idea seems to be that something which is rooted originally in practice and shared sentiment may gradually take on a life of its own as a worldly normative reality.

It is possible to make the mistake of thinking of positive law as an all-or-nothing affair: either a set of norms exists as positive law or it doesn't. But positive law, particularly in its customary forms (which include the customary foundations of any viable system of command)[28] often emerges, which means that its existence as law can be a matter of degree. It does not simply spring into existence. We sometimes obscure things more than we illuminate them by insisting on crisp answers to the sort of ontological questions that Professor Benhabib poses: is this law or is it morality? There is a risk that by posing the question too sharply we may underestimate both the positive presence and the jurisgenerative potential of a body of human interaction and practice.

Here's an analogy. Professor Benhabib began her lectures with a reminder of Hannah Arendt's initial skepticism about the category of "crimes against humanity." That, as we have seen, was a productive starting point. But it is instructive, too, to see how badly wrong Arendt was in her assessment of another related area of norms, when she approached it with categories of analysis that were too rigid or that ignored the question of what a normative order looks like as it is *beginning* to come into positive existence. I refer here to Arendt's terrible underestimation of the growth of the human rights movement. In 1951 in *The Origins of Totalitarianism,* Arendt wrote this about what had been going on in the contemporary growth of human rights law:

All attempts to arrive at a new bill of human rights were sponsored by marginal figures – by a few international jurists without political experience or professional philanthropists supported by the uncertain sentiments of professional idealists. The groups they formed, the declarations they issued, showed an uncanny similarity in language and composition to that of societies for the prevention of cruelty to animals. No statesman, no political figure of any importance could possibly take them seriously.[29]

Now this was written just as international human rights law was beginning to grow out of what she was dismissing—in a Burkean spirit—as "chaff and rags, and paltry blurred shreds of paper about the rights of man."[30] It consisted largely at the time of what we now call "soft law"—diplomatic declarations and assurances, a patchwork of treaties and conventions subscribed to by some states and not others, the sentiments and expressions of concern recorded at public meetings, the proceedings of conferences, miscellaneous protocols, the deliverances of tribunals whose status was unclear, and so on. Hannah Arendt can perhaps be forgiven for not foreseeing that this would in fact grow, fifty years later, into the dense thicket of human rights law whose influence is felt in every corner of the legal world. But we should not so readily forgive her for urging her readers to approach the earliest stages of this development with categories that simply assume that if we cannot already identify the hard outlines of familiar legal institutions, we should dismiss a body of practice that *aspires* to juridical status as mere claptrap. The successful coming-into-being of human rights law was not a fore-ordained conclusion; but Arendt missed the point that if it were to come into being, this is what its earliest stages would look like, and that its coming-into-being would involve not the thunderous imposition of positive law from on high but the accretion and gradual crystallization of materials such as these.

Returning now from the analogy to the cosmopolitan norms themselves, I think there are elements in Professor Benhabib's second lecture that can help illuminate this "jurisgenerative" process and avoid the rigidity of an Arendtian skepticism. In considering the emergence of norms of toleration and identity in a European context, Benhabib invites us to make use of Jacques Derrida's concept of "iteration," by which she means the process involved in the repeated use of a given concept, whereby each use never simply replicates but varies and enriches the concept that is repeatedly invoked:

The iteration and interpretation of norms . . . is never merely an act of repetition. Every iteration involves making sense of an authoritative original in a new and different context. The antecedent thereby is reposited and resignified via subsequent usages and references. Meaning is enhanced and transformed.... Iteration is the reappropriation of the "origin"; it is at the same time its dissolution as the original and its preservation through its continuous deployment (48).

Benhabib is particularly interested in the way in which the transformation of norms under iteration might be conceived as "democratic" even though the change has not formally been put to a vote. It is democratic simply in the demotic dailiness of its use and iterated modification. (And I would add: the *emergence* of norms out of practice, as well as their transformation, can be seen in this light as well.) I think this idea is extremely important in understanding connections between positive law and democratic legitimacy— connections that don't necessarily involve formal legislative enactment. Custom too can seem democratic because of the embeddedness of its dynamic in the daily lives and interactions of ordinary people.[31] Of course, if one is willing to make this connection, one has to loosen the link between democratic legitimacy and the idea of a decision-procedure strictly regimented by political equality (in the way that voting is). A norm's transformation can be described as democratic, not because a change was approved by people voting as equals, but because the change emerged from the dynamics of ordinary life in relation to which there have been no problematic or invidious exclusions. Our theory of this is as yet undeveloped. But Professor Benhabib's thoughts on iteration in the second lecture are a major contribution.

Let me add two final points. First, in illustrating these processes of democratic iteration, it is no doubt interesting to focus on high-profile issues such as public discussion of *l'affaire du foulard* in France. But, as I said earlier, it is equally important to focus on the high-frequency but lower-profile uses and repetitions of norms in the mundane density of ordinary life. If we really want to understand how the world is coming to be ordered by cosmopolitan norms, we have to look at the ordinary as well as the extraordinary, the tedious as well as the exciting, the commercial as well as the ideological.

The second point is that by shifting our attention away from formal democratic legitimacy to the more demotic legitimacy of ordinary iteration, we need not be as preoccupied as we are in traditional legal and political theory with borders and the scope of norms. Norms emerge in the world in the circumstances of dense interaction that occur *all over the place.* The conditions of their existence and identity are unrelated to boundaries; we need no longer think in those terms. If this is right, then I think Professor Benhabib can afford to drop or at least moderate her talk of a "theoretical dilemma" in relation to cosmopolitan order—the dilemma is supposed to consist in the fact that "universalist norms are mediated with the self-understanding of local communities" (71). There is no dilemma. No doubt each incident, each use or iteration of a cosmopolitan norm takes place somewhere. But its location has no political or juridical significance. It takes place in the world and its effect—or the effect of thousands like it—is felt in the world. There may be other reasons for wanting to continue placing theoretical emphasis on the local or the national or the communal, but the problem of the provenance of cosmopolitan norms is not one of them. They emerge in the world, they are iterated and transformed in the world, and they apply to the world—all in the lives of ordinary people dealing with one another, with friends and with strangers, without preconceived ideas of who's in or who's out of their circle.

Notes

1. There is a similar classification in Samuel Scheffler, "Conceptions of Cosmopolitanism," in his collection *Boundaries and Allegiances: Problems of Justice and Responsibility in Liberal Thought* (Oxford: Oxford University Press, 2001). In each case, Scheffler also draws a distinction between "strong" and "moderate" versions of cosmopolitanism.

2. See Jeremy Waldron, "Minority Cultures and the Cosmopolitan Alternative," in Will Kymlicka (ed.), *The Rights of Minority Cultures* (Oxford: Oxford University Press, 1995), p. 93.

3. There is an immense law review literature on social norms. See, for a review, Richard McAdams, "The Origin, Development, and Regulation of Norms," *Michigan Law Review* 96 (1997) 338. See also Robert C. Ellickson, *Order Without Law: How Neighbors Settle Disputes* (Cambridge, Mass.: Harvard University Press, 1991).

4. I shall follow the convention among jurists and call national law (like the law of France or the state and federal law of the United States) "municipal" law. (It has nothing necessarily to do with the governance of small cities (municipalities).

5. See, for example, Anne-Marie Slaughter, *A New World Order* (Princeton, N.J.: Princeton University Press, 2004). Consider also the controversy over the citation of foreign and international law in U.S. constitutional cases: for instance in *Roper v. Simmonds* 125 S.Ct. 1183 (2005), at 1198–1200 (per curiam) and 1225–1229 (Scalia, J., dissenting).

6. Of course there are differences. But the differences are as often differences between various international or regional conventions, or differences between various national Bills of Rights, as they are differences between a given item from the national level and a given international convention.

7. Jean-Jacques Rousseau, *The Social Contract and Other Later Political Writings*, ed. Victor Gourevitch (Cambridge: Cambridge University Press, 1997), p. 67: "[W]hen the whole people enacts statutes for the whole people it considers only itself, and if a relation is formed, it is between the entire object from one point of view, and the entire object from another point of view, with no division of the whole. Then the matter with regard to which the statute is being enacted is general, as is the enacting will. It is this act which I call law. . . . [L]aw combines the universality of the will and that of the object."

8. Immanuel Kant, *Toward Perpetual Peace* (1795) and *The Metaphysics of Morals* (1797) in *Practical Philosophy* (in the Cambridge edition of the Works of Immanuel Kant), edited by Mary J. Gregor (Cambridge: Cambridge University Press, 1996). For ease of reference, all citations to Kant's work will be by volume and page number of the Prussian Academy edition of Kant's *Werke* as well as by page number to Mary Gregor's Cambridge edition.

9. Kant, *Perpetual Peace*, op. cit., pp. 328–329 (8: 357–358).

10. Ibid., p. 328 (8: 357).

11. It is like one of Dworkin's legal principles: see Ronald Dworkin, Taking Rights Seriously (Cambridge, Mass.: Harvard University press, 1978), pp. 22–45. See also, for this reading of hospitality, Jeremy Waldron, "What is Cosmopolitan?" *Journal of Political Philosophy* 8 (2000): 227.

12. Compare Michel Foucault on reading Nietzsche, in *Power/ Knowledge: Selected Interviews and Other Writings 1972–1977*, edited by Colin Gordon (New York: Pantheon Books, 1980), pp. 53–54: "For myself, I prefer to *utilize* the writers I like. The only valid tribute to thought such as Nietzsche's is precisely to use it, to deform it, to make it groan and protest. And if commentators then say that I am being faithful or unfaithful to Nietzsche, that is of absolutely no interest."

13. Immanuel Kant, On the Common Saying: That may be Correct in Theory, but it is of no Use in Practice, in *Practical Philosophy*, op. cit., p. 307 (8:310).

14. Kant, Metaphysics of Morals, op. cit., pp. 482 and 489 (6: 343 and 352).

15. Kant, On the Common Saying . . . , op. cit., p. 307 (8: 310).

16. Kant, Perpetual Peace, op. cit., pp. 329–330 (8: 358–359).

17. Ibid., p. 329 (8: 358).

18. See, e.g., Kwame Anthony Appiah, *The Ethics of Identity* (Princteon, N.J.: Princeton University Press, 2004).

19. We sometimes imagine a pristine world of anthropologically isolated societies, each enjoying their own culture. In fact, historically and prehistorically the default position has been more or less exactly the contrary: intense interaction, and the existence of traditions, cultures, and institutions of interaction, among all societies whenever interaction is a possibility. Societies that can interact do. This is how they form themselves as well their in-between. The myth of pure independence applies at most only to those few societies where, for geographical reasons, cultural interchange with others was (for a period) never in the cards.

20. Kant, Perpetual Peace, op. cit., pp. 329–330 (8: 359).

21. Jeremy Waldron, "Alternatives to Nationalism: Proximity and Conflict as the Bassi of a State" (2005 Daniel Jacobson Lecture, Hebrew University of Jerusalem), forthcoming *Israel Law Review*. See also Jeremy Waldron, "Kant's Legal Positivism," *Harvard Law Review* 109 (1996):1535.

22. Kant, On the Common Saying . . . , op. cit., p. 308 (8: 311).

23. Sophocles, *Antigone*, 499–501.

24. H. L. A. Hart, *The Concept of Law*, 2nd ed. (Oxford: Clarendon Press, 1994), esp. chaps. 5–6.

25. For a good discussion of the development of the law merchant, see Harold J. Berman, *Law and Revolution: The Formation of the Western Legal Tradition* (Cambridge, Mass.: Harvard University Press, 1983), pp. 333–356. Berman emphasizes (Ibid., p. 342) that in the medieval and early modern period, "[t]ransnational trade often predominated over local trade and provided an important model for commercial transactions," and that contemporary writers emphasized that it was uniform between jurisdictions and "not a law established by the sovereignty of any prince" (idem). For the situation in the modern world, see the discussion in Keith Highet, "The Enigma of the Lex Mercatoria," *Tulane Law Review* 63 (1989): 613.

26. Kant, Perpetual Peace, op. cit., pp. 329–330 (8: 358–359).

27. Ibid., p. 330 (8: 360).

28. Hart, op. cit.

29. Hannah Arendt, *The Origins of Totalitarianism* (New York: Harcourt, Brace, 1951), p. 289.

30. Edmund Burke, *Reflections on the Revolution in France*, edited by Conor Cruise O'Brien (Harmondsworth: Penguin Books, 1965), p. 182; cf. Arendt's invocation of Burke in *Origins*, op. cit., p. 295.

31. I have pursued this idea in Jeremy Waldron, *Law and Disagreement* (Oxford: Clarendon Press, 1999), pp. 55–68.

Another Cosmopolitanism? Law and Politics in the New Europe

Bonnie Honig

In *Another Cosmopolitanism*, Seyla Benhabib celebrates recent developments in the institutionalization and juridification of what she calls cosmopolitan norms. She treats genocide as a synecdoche for several new legislative and normative trends in human rights, especially in Europe.[1] The naming of genocide, as such, she says, puts us into a "new normative universe . . . even . . . into a universe which now contains a new moral fact—'Thou shalt not commit genocide and perpetrate crimes against humanity'" (73). But why is this new moral fact here articulated in the old moral form of divine prohibition?[2] Benhabib's *Another Cosmopolitanism* seeks to reclaim universalism (20, 69) for a postmetaphysical politics, but her reclamation is marked by traces of earlier universalisms that promise moral guidance from above to a wayward human world below.

Benhabib opens and closes these lectures by invoking Hannah Arendt, the democratic theorist to whom she and I are both, in different ways, very much indebted. The Hannah Arendt with whom she opens is in dialogue with Jaspers in 1960 regarding the need (shared by Jaspers and Arendt but felt more keenly by him) for international institutions to try Eichmann for war crimes. Arendt's hesitations about the "impaired" (her term) quality of the justice meted out at Nuremberg and then at the Eichmann trial in Jerusalem are overcome in these lectures by Benhabib, who casts the establishment of the new International Criminal Court in 2002 as itself a fulfillment of the promise of those initial, partial efforts and as an instance of the sort of inaugural action that Arendt theorized and praised in *The Human Condition, On Revolution* and elsewhere. This is the second Arendt, the Arendt with whom Benhabib closes, the theorist of revolutionary beginnings who sees politics as an opportunity for actors to inaugurate a *"novo ordo saeclorum."*[3]

But would the Arendt who expressed concerns about the impaired quality of the Eichmann trial have agreed with Benhabib's assessment of the new normative and juridical universalism endorsed here? True, Arendt bemoaned the absence of appropriate institutions with which to try Eichmann. And she did criticize the Israeli court for trying Eichmann on the wrong charge—crimes against the Jewish people rather than crimes against humanity. This may be why Benhabib believes that the new international court along with the new moral fact—prohibiting crimes against humanity—together answer to Arendt's earlier concerns. But Arendt's analysis of the Eichmann trial did not stop there. These two criticisms are part and parcel of a third, in which Arendt not only noted the imperfections of the trial, but also tracked the trial's political functions. She asked not only "How are they trying Eichmann?" but also always: "What are they doing by trying Eichmann? What political ends is this trial serving?" This, indeed, is what offended many of her readers; that she would dare to suggest that the State of Israel might be operating politically, that it would *use* this trial, that the trial was not an end in itself, that it was a quest for something other than absolute, unconditional justice.

Arendt was relentlessly insistent on the politicality of the trial. For her, the Eichmann trial, in spite of the fact that it was needed and not completely invalid but only impaired, nonetheless operated to some extent like a show trial: Through it, the still-new Israeli state sought its own legitimation as a nation state by casting itself as protector of international Jewry and seeker of justice for the crimes of the Holocaust. It is in this context that her other two criticisms—wrong charges (crimes against the Jewish people), wrong setting (Israeli court in Jerusalem)—are significant. The trial provided the State of Israel with an opportunity further to nationalize itself as a state, and this dealt yet another blow to Arendt's dashed dream for a binational state of Israel in which Palestinians and Jews would share power. This is the reason for Arendt's scathing criticisms of Gideon Hausner in the early pages of *Eichmann in Jerusalem*. Indeed, her half-hearted wish for an international criminal court, expressed in the form of a lamentation of its impossibility, was not simply a wish to escape from politics as such into a really neutral or just realm of law. Or that's not all it was. It was (whatever else it was) a way to highlight and criticize the part played by the Eichmann trial in a larger politics of state-building to which she was opposed.

So the question is: Would Hannah Arendt—if she were writing now-have any less political an analysis of the formation of the EU and the use therein of law, courts, bureaucracy, and trials to promote and consolidate a particular conception of Europe as a political form? Would she be any less likely now than then to ask not just "what can we accomplish through law on behalf of human rights?" but also "what new political formations are being advantaged and legitimated thereby?" Her example suggests not. It suggests that she would assess new international norms, laws, and institutions not simply as good or bad solutions to an earlier problem but *also* always as political maneuvers in their own right. In this particular instance, I imagine she would see the developments tracked in Benhabib's lectures as signs of welcome developments in human rights. But Arendt would not stop there. She would, I believe, also see these developments as part of an effort to consolidate a certain conception of Europe and promote it over other contenders. Thus, rather than treat the Arendt who wished for appropriate international institutions to judge Eichmann as if she were fulfilled or satisfied by the inauguration of today's new norms and institutions, we might do better to see in Arendt's example an invitation to assess emerging new orders in the most relentlessly political and critical terms. In particular, Arendt offers a valuable example of the double gesture often called for in political engagement when she criticizes the politicality of the Eichmann trial while nonetheless affirming its justice. (In this regard, it would be worthwhile to compare her judgment of the Eichmann trial to Kant's judgment of the French Revolution, mediated by his faith in progress.[4])

In the pages that follow, I look at the recent developments in Europe focused on by Benhabib, but I do so from an alternative perspective that owes much to Arendt's political analysis in *Eichmann* and is indebted as well to the work of Jacques Derrida. I begin with Derrida's own reading of the right to hospitality, for it motivates an alternative to Benhabib's neo-Kantian cosmopolitanism, one that, for lack of a better word, is often termed *cosmopolitics*.[5]

As with many of the other concepts he deconstructs, including the gift, justice, forgiveness, and democracy, Derrida casts hospitality as belonging to two, discontinuous and radically heterogeneous orders, conditional and unconditional, whose conflict and asymmetrical necessity render ethical-political life (im)possible (*Rogues*, 145). There is no question of a choice that must be made between one order and the other, between the conditional and the unconditional. Nor is there a fundamental compatibility between the two such that, for example, one is political and the other moral, or one is specific and the other generic, in which case the latter could subsume the former and make sense of it or complete it. Rather, the two orders or concepts co-exist in "paradoxical or aporetic relations . . . that are at once heterogeneous and inseparable."[6]

Unconditional hospitality postulates a giving without limit to the other, an infinite openness that both enables and jeopardizes one's capacity to host another (*Adieu*, 47, *Of Hospitality*, 25–27). Conditional hospitality, by contrast, postulates a finite set of resources and calculable claims. It is "the only one . . . that belongs to the order of laws, rules, and norms—whether ethical, juridical, or political—at a national or international level" (*Rogues*, 173 n. 12). In this second order of hospitality, distinctions must be made and limits set, lest hospitality be extended to or demanded by everyone and encompass everything to a point at which the would-be host would be dispossessed of the very property and scope that enable him to offer hospitality to the dispossessed other.

Kant delimited hospitality (to the right of those washed ashore to be permitted visitation or offered refuge) precisely in order to avert this risk of dispossession and thereby secure, by limiting it, the duty of (conditional) hospitality. Derrida, by contrast, insists that we see what the averted risk itself intimates, that against which we cannot inoculate ourselves: That those who claim a right to hospitality position their hosts inevitably in an ambiguous and undecidable terrain marked by both hospitality and hostility. The undecidability of host/hostility and its ethicopolitical implications are erased, not captured, by an analysis like Benhabib's that insistently identifies *hostility* with one singular principle—ethnos, or republican self-determination, or state nationalism-and *hospitality* with another that is distinct and apart—Enlightenment universalism. The division of host/hostility into two distinct and opposed binary options misleadingly casts the threat to universal hospitality as something that always comes to it from some distinct and unrelated outside—to wit: hostility.[7] The mutual implication of host/hostility, by contrast, illustrates the persistent trace even in our own most cherished ideals of that which we seek to overcome.

Any right to hospitality is caught in the aporia signaled by the two orders, the one heterogeneous to the other, and yet necessary in some way to it. And, Derrida points out, although "*unconditional* hospitality [is] impossible, . . . heterogeneous to the political, the juridical, and even the ethical . . . the impossible is not nothing. It is even that which happens, which comes, by definition" (*Rogues*, 172 n. 12). One way to think (part of) this thought might be as follows: Any particular right to hospitality takes its motivation, its energy and animation, not just from a finite economy of right nor just from a moral law, universal human rights, or particularist ethics, but also and problematically from the infinitude of the unconditional hospitality that is both expressed and betrayed by any proclaimed table of values (whether legal or moral), by any enacted right to or gift of hospitality as such.

The distinction between the unconditional and the conditional might illuminate from a new angle Arendt's famous call for *the right to have rights.* This is a call in the name of an unconditional order of rights, something that is quite distinct, as she herself makes clear in her reading of *Billy Budd* and elsewhere, from such tables of rights as universal human rights, the Rights of Man, or EU charters. The right to have rights is itself a double gesture: it is a reproach to any particular order of rights (albeit certainly to some more than others) *and* a demand that everyone should belong to one such order.[8] A double gesture is necessary because, paradoxically, we need rights because we cannot trust the political communities to which we belong to treat us with dignity and respect; however, we depend for our rights on those very same political communities. Are we helped out of the paradox by locating the ground of rights in a different, higher order of belonging, such as international institutions? Yes and no. Having another place to go to appeal when you lose in one venue is invariably a good thing. But being able to so appeal presupposes the belonging whose fragility those very same rights are supposed to protect us against. In the international arena no less than in the national, rights still presuppose belonging, now not only to states, but also (in Benhabib's depiction) to a legal, bureaucratic and administrative order or to the EU. International institutions, courts and arbitration boards do not dispense with the need for membership; they just change the venue of membership (for good reason, given the violence of which states are capable, but why expect better performances from international institutions? Perhaps here the weakness of those institutions—their lack of serious police and military power [for the moment]—is their strength).

The unconditional—Arendt's right to have rights—is a way of marking the fact that no armory of rights (conditional, contingent), no matter how broad or developed or secure, can represent the subject's absolute value in the intersubjective, contingent realm of rights-adjudication, a realm that is at once communal, legal, judicial, moral, bureaucratic, administrative, governmental, and discretionary. And there is no way out of the paradox of rights, although awareness of it can inflect our politics in useful ways. Indeed, Arendt's right to have rights—a polemical, political call—directs our attention repeatedly to the need for a *politics* whereby to express and address the paradox as it is experienced by minorities, the stateless, the powerless, and the hapless.

Benhabib agrees. She also wants to generate a politics in response to a paradox that she wants *not* to resolve. But her version—democratic iterations—is different from the one explored here. In particular, it generates different diagnoses of our current situation. From a vantage point shaped by awareness of the conditional/unconditional, and modeled on Arendt's own analysis of the Eichmann trial, things look more ambiguous than on Benhabib's account. For example, although Benhabib is right to point out the great promise for democratic citizens in the development of Europe's newly porous borders, in new recognitions of extracitizen human rights and alien (but still membership-based) suffrage, and in extrastate fora to which state-based injustices can be appealed, it is also the case that a focus on these developments can be seriously misleading; also misleading is the casting of these developments as signs of an increasingly capacious normative universalism.[9] The new porousness of territorial borders among EU countries has been accompanied in recent years by the erection of new, not at all porous borders inside the EU. The hosts are not only welcoming; they are also hostile.

And this is no accident. As postcolonial immigrants exercise their option in recent years for French citizenship or legal residency, those who do not fit the profile of the proper citizen are subjected by formal and informal state agents to police or administrative control and informal intimidation. When policed postcolonial subjects, only some of them sans papiers, are constantly asked for their papers, this renders fraught and fragile the place of all postcolonial immigrants, residents, and ethnic minorities on the territory to which some of them are now said to belong, in some sense, under French and EU law. Is it not significant that, at a time of new economic pressures a new class of worker is created, an always already criminalized population that is unable to access the resources of law and rights that are at that moment expanded? Criminalized populations are often quiescent.

But they sometimes take the risk (riskier for them than most) of politics, as the sans papiers movement has demonstrated. What that movement also demonstrated is the fact that in practice if not in law, French residents are now repartitioned not along the formal juridical line—undocumented/documented—but along racial lines. Many are moved by the situation to joke cynically that their cartes d'identites are their faces, their skin/color. Etienne Balibar is moved to name the new racialized political order "apartheid in Europe."[10] In this Europe, formal law lives side by side with, but is also both aided and undercut by, an administrative police-state apparatus and a xenophobic public that legalists disavow at their (and our) peril, as Arendt herself pointed out insightfully about an earlier Europe, before World War I and after World War II.[11]

And yet, for the most part, Benhabib focuses in her second lecture on formal law, on state and regional powers, commissions' rulings and Court decisions.[12] She has a formalist's understanding of law: "The law provides the framework within which the work of culture and politics go on. The laws, as the ancients knew, are the walls of the city, but the art and passions of politics occur within those walls and very often politics leads to the breaking down of these barriers or at least to assuring their permeability" (60). This call to break down the barriers between law and politics by way of politics is not antiformalist: Although it seems to attenuate law's independence from politics, it also thereby secures that independence by positing a chronology in which law is, first, prior to politics and capable therefore of providing a framework for it; then, second, law is corrupted by politics, and finally law is brought into the political arena in order to wrest from it (in its limited democratic or republican form) payment on its universal (context-transcendent, i.e. extrapolitical) promise: "It is only when new groups claim that they belong within the circles of addressees of a right from which they have been excluded in its initial articulation that we come to understand the fundamental limitedness of every rights claim within a constitutional tradition as well as its context-transcending validity" (60).

This view of rights as always pointing (or made to point) beyond themselves is deeply attractive. However, what those rights point to in Benhabib's account is not an open futurity dotted by new or emergent rights but a normative validity that launches us into a subsumptive logic in which new claims are assessed not in terms of the new worlds they may bring into being but rather in terms of their appositeness to molds and models already in place: incomplete, but definitive in their contours. Benhabib notes this but does not seem troubled by it: "It is clear that all future struggles with respect to the rights of Muslim and other immigrants will be fought within the framework created by the universalistic principles of Europe's commitments to human rights, on the one hand [but what evidence could put their universality in doubt? What principle?], and the exigencies of democratic self-determination on the other" (61).[13] With Europe's commitments cast as universalistic, (in theory if not in practice, Benhabib might concede; but then something in her theory prevents the practice—racial stratification, police-state–style policing, and so on—from being seen as significant evidence regarding the theory), there is little room to take seriously the sort of concern aired by Derrida in *Of Hospitality*: "the foreigner who, inept at speaking the language, always risks being without defense before the law of the country [or region] that welcomes or expels him; the foreigner is first of all foreign to the legal language in which the duty of hospitality is formulated, the right to asylum, its limits, norms, policing, etc. He has to ask for hospitality in a language which by definition is not his own . . ." (15).

On Benhabib's account, this foreigner is always already marked as particularity in relation to European universality. And although she treats both as two moments in a dialectic, the two are not equal: Universality represents *a principle*; democratic self-determination an *exigency*. And universality provides the perspective from which the claims of particularity are judged. This is quite different from a formulation like Derrida's, which seeks to underline the *alienness* of a universalism that seeks to subsume the new or the foreign under categories whose fundamental character and validity are unchanged or unaffected by this encounter between newcomer and established rules or norms. Notwithstanding her commitments to reflexivity and revisability (written about in detail elsewhere), what changes in Benhabib's practices of democratic iteration here, notably, is the subject's relation to universalistic categories, not the categories themselves, (the universal stays universal, the particular stays particular), nor the picture of rights-claiming as, per se, a practice wherein newcomers petition for subsumption or recognition under existing categories.

More to the point, this model of rights adjudication as a practice of subsumption itself presupposes a certain linear and progressive temporality and that temporality does quite a lot of unacknowledged work in Benhabib's argument. It reassures us that continued developments along the trajectory of rights will take us to a desirable democratic outcome. The unconditional, by contrast, makes no promise to us about our future, and it inspires and haunts every conditional order of rights. From its vantage point, we wager that remainders will always result from every political-legal settlement, no matter how progressive or expansive, even, as it were, from the instantiation of the universal itself. (This is in no way to suggest that all orders are equal from this perspective; only to suggest that even those that are better than others still depend upon the supplement of a politics that is different from Benhabib's iterative politics.) From the vantage point of the unconditional but not from that of Benhabib's universal, for example, even a full realization of universal human rights on earth would be seen as necessitating further political work, generating new claims, each of which would make its own universal appeal, perhaps on behalf of those forms of life remaindered by the order of universal human rights, which is itself a conditional order. (Benhabib by contrast would see such further claims as coming from a particularity in need of education, adjustment.) Put a different way: If we expect hospitality always to harbor a trace of its double—hostility— then proponents of hospitality will always be on the lookout for that trace and its remainders. The same goes for universalism or cosmopolitanism. And that wariness will surface in our politics, often in the form of a double gesture, in which the promises *and* risks of a particular conditional order of hospitality (and universalism or cosmopolitanism) are both named and confronted.

Benhabib makes no such double gestures. Here the work performed by her assumption of progressive, linear temporality is most noticeable, as when she points out that, over time, second class members of democratic regimes like women and African Americans have been brought into full possession of formal rights. She does not also note that these subjects have still never come to bear those rights in the same way as their original bearers. There is evolutionary temporality in her discussion of Marshall (who himself uses evolutionary language) and in her own characterization of the second class status of colonial American Jews as "transitional" (en route to what?) in the first lecture (34). This is a tempting narration, and a familiar one, in which supposed systems of rights are (to borrow Habermas's term) "tapped" as liberal democracies take the protections and privileges they first limited to propertied white males and then spread them outward to encompass all classes, races and genders. It is from this perspective that the status of colonial Jews looks transitional. But that is not how colonial Jews would have described their status, surely. Here Benhabib adopts the backward-looking gaze of one who knows already (or hopes) that universal human rights will win out over democratic particularity in the end. That perspective is evident as well when Benhabib wagers that the three girls from Creil who talked back to the French state will one day learn as well to talk back to Islam (67).

Evolutionary time obscures from view the fact that others, resident aliens for example, have been *dis*enfranchised along the way. Alien suffrage used to be an accepted, uncontroversial practice, in the United States and Canada, until the practice was ended by World War I—era xenophobia. Historically, alien suffrage occurred without all the things that Benhabib sets up as necessitating it now: border attenuation, pressures on state sovereignty and extranational institutions.[14] Faced with the prior practice of alien suffrage, it is hard to think of recent gains in alien suffrage as the latest in a line of serial expansions earned by our progressive tapping of the system of rights.[15] Without a linear temporality structuring our view, alien suffrage becomes a historically contested practice, sometimes won, sometimes lost, and always possessed of different meanings—sometimes nationalist, sometimes universalist—in different, conditional contexts. For example, is it insignificant that when the idea of alien suffrage appealed to the province of Schleswig-Holstein in 1989, the aliens to be empowered to vote were all citizens of Northern European countries while the new minorities putting the most pressure on traditional German conceptions of citizenship at the time were from the more liminal borderland of Turkey? And is it not significant that recent debates in Europe about the social rights of aliens, specifically about whether "we" should share our social welfare with "them," have occurred in the last two decades at the very moment at which European social welfare rights have been downsized? Depictions of foreigners as those who want to come "here" to take "our" welfare have worked to reassure western Europeans that they still have social welfare worth taking (which they may, by comparison with others, but which they do not, by comparison with themselves thirty years ago).

Where the unconditional focuses our gaze on the remainders of new and established orders, Benhabib sees those remainders but does not assess them as such, that is, as *remainders*. She knows that at the very moment in which "the entitlement to rights is" expanded, "the condition of undocumented aliens, as well as of refugees and asylum seekers . . . remains in that murky domain between legality and illegality" (46), but she does not read this remnant as a *remainder produced by* the conditional order of universal hospitality (as I myself have been suggesting it is; though other forces unnoted here are at work, too). Instead, her language suggests, the problem is that some people have been left passively behind by an imperfect but still progressive cosmopolitan law, in which case appeals to human rights commissions and exercises of cultural political interventions may correct the wrong and result in a truer universalism. She subtly puts us onto a temporal register in which this limit is always already about to be overcome. From that register, we are in no position to ask whether these remainders are the direct products of the political project of Europe-formation which is, we might note, not only a vehicle whereby national belonging is transcended, but also a way to resecure national belonging: In a time when claims to national belonging, say, in France, are being made by non-Europeans, the political (re)formation of Europe as a site of belonging is surely a way to resecure and not just attenuate or transcend national belonging. As Derrida points out in *The Other Heading*: "I am (we are) all the more national for being European, all the more European for being trans-European, and international..." (48). The challenge then is to see the situation in all its ambiguity and from that vantage point to intervene in ways that claim Europe for a different present and future, for different constituencies, for a different politics. The challenge is to open up room for the much-needed double gesture: for example, to oppose the constitutionalization of the EU in the name of an alternative locatable and accountable rule of law, to counter that future with another in the name of the very democratic and human rights that constitutionalization has historically *claimed* to entrench, and to do all this without being cast as a mere agonist, or a defender of national particularity, or as a member of the National Front, as if these were the only options (naysayer vs. lawgiver; NF or EU).

That same challenge lurks in Benhabib's treatment of sovereignty. Here the very same evidence that allows her to speculate hopefully but cautiously that "the conflict between *sovereignty* and *hospitality* has weakened in intensity" (47) could also suggest that sovereignty is in the process of being shored up, transformed into something altogether new. The new openness Benhabib endorses can just as well be a sign of sovereignty's adjustments, accommodations, and relocations—from visible peripheral borders to less visible internal ones (city/suburbs, French/Algerian, Catholic/Moslem/Jewish/secular), from states to regions or from states weakened by globalization to states re-empowered by their new, sometimes fraught membership in regional associations, like Europe, which restore nationalist fervor or salvage it while also perhaps attenuating or redirecting it, and working to secure the continent's peripheral borders in ways that mime the old state sovereignties.[16] Just as the problem of refugees, to which Benhabib briefly alludes, may not be (just) a *problem* for state sovereignty but rather *or also*, as Nevzat Soguk argues, an *occasion* for the refinement and enhancement of state power, so, too, the problem of refugeeism in Europe, testified to by the many refugee camps lined up on both sides of Europe's old and new borders, may serve as a sign of the new continental sovereignty of the EU.[17] Here, Giorgio Agamben's suggestion regarding state sovereignty may motivate a new analysis as well of the EU: What if refugees, rather than (or in addition to) being the exceptions of the juridical state (or continental) system, are metaphorically its norm, the exemplary objects of the sort of power that the state system and its sovereign legalism represent but hide— Bio-power and its rule over all as bare life?[18]

Benhabib says she is led to cosmopolitanism by the new empirical facts of state sovereignty attenuation in the late twentieth century. A lot *has* changed in recent years. But the 'facts' are not univocal; they can be variously perceived and interpreted (as I have been demonstrating here). Indeed, Benhabib's turn to cosmopolitanism seems to me to have been in some sense overdetermined by other factors. Long before cosmopolitan norms were on their agenda, Habermas and his followers sought a solution to the paradox of democratic legitimation, (what happens when the people on whose will the legitimacy of a regime rests will the wrong thing?), another version of which serves as Benhabib's point of departure here. They found that solution in various forms of statism (including the rule of law), which they relied upon to preserve deliberative democratic norms and procedures from the caprice of the people, or local majorities. Concerns about the undemocratic nature of the statist solution got vented in the 1990s by way of analyses of the paradox of constitutional democracy, a paradox that in failing to name the state, as such, as a problem for democracy, covered over the real concern while also giving some vent to it.[19] Because there are now concerns about the state's caprice—most especially about state-sponsored violence and injustice—a new paradox of democratic legitimation, which pits cosmopolitanism norms against republican self-determination, surfaces as the problem that has to be solved in these lectures. (All of Benhabib's examples in the second lecture are of state-based injustices agitated against by local and transnational agents and agencies.) But although it surfaces as a problem, the new paradox of democratic legitimation is really also working as a solution, the solution to the last paradox's now problematic solution: statism. In short, at each register, universalism (or rights, as I noted earlier) seeks a new harbor: liberalism, constitutionalism, state institutions, and now — cosmopolitanism. But no harbor is safe. (Sound familiar? It is the story Hegel tells in the *Philosophy of Right*.) That is, of course, because the universal is never really as we imagine it: truly unconditional, context-transcending, and unmarked by particularity and politics.

In the end, statism is not really overcome. Benhabib applauds three girls from Creil for having learned to "talk back to the state" (67). (The applause is to some extent contingent, however, on the likelihood that they will therefore learn also one day to talk back to Islam.) But those three girls from Creil did not act alone; they were fronts for an organization, a social movement, represented in Benhabib's text by M. Daniel Youssef Leclerq, head of Integrite and former president of the National Federation of Muslims in France. This is for Benhabib an indication that the girls' gesture was a "conscious political" one (53). That may be. But it also indicates something else: the girls appeared in the public realm as the effects of a social movement, no less than Rosa Parks did when she supposedly spontaneously one day out of the blue simply refused to move to the back of the bus. It is a trick and a victory of statist law and politics in liberal democracies to ascribe to individuals those significant actions that are actually (also) the products of a concerted politics. Rival sovereignties, oppositional movements, and political dissidence are thereby erased from view and we are left only with small individuals (three girls) or large phantoms (Islam, radical particularism, etc.). Benhabib nicely unpacks some of the complexities at work here. But she does not dwell on the role of social movements in these cases of "democratic iteration," and absent that it is hard to tell what's democratic about them.[20]

An alternative democratic cosmopolitics, oriented by the unconditional order of hospitality, might join Benhabib on several fronts, including her endorsement of the reinhabitation of the French Marianne by postcolonial (im)migrants. But such a politics might also unsettle elements of her universal human rights agenda. For example, it might adopt a hyperlegalist critique of state violence in the name of the rule of law while also resisting the legalists' project of constitutionalizing the EU. These seemingly contradictory moves are made in the name of those human rights more likely to be attenuated than secured by the EU's constitutional order and in the name of a more engaged, accountable democratic politics than that thus far identified with the EU, hampered until now by the famous "democratic deficit" that goes unmentioned in these lectures.[21] Such a double gesture is characteristic of what I would name an "agonistic cosmopolitics" by contrast with the subsumptive normative cosmopolitanism on which Benhabib's democratic iterations are premised.

An agonistic cosmopolitics locates itself squarely in the paradox of founding, that irresolvable and productive paradox in which a future is claimed on behalf of peoples and rights that are not yet and may never be. Arendt's unconditional right to have rights is as good a motto as any for that project, as long as we understand rights to imply a world-building that is not incompatible with the project of building juridical institutions and safeguards, but also reaches beyond that project because it is wary of the sedimentations of power and discretion that accrete in such institutional contexts. In the name of such a right to have rights and motivated by the doubly gestured diagnoses developed here of in/formal law and politics as they are now operating in Europe, an agonistic cosmopolitics might call for: the enactment of underground railroads devoted to the remainders of the state system, such as refugees (Michael Rogin);[22] or the designation of some spaces as cities of refuge, (but not camps), such as Jacques Derrida called for (following the recovery of them by Immanuel Levinas, who commented on the biblical injunction to establish six of these in Israel); or we might stand up for droits de cite, a demand to extend full hospitality to refugees and other non-immigrant border crossers simply because they are here. We can enact *droits de cité*—by taking people in, harboring them, offering them shelter, finding sympathetic agents of discretionary power who are willing to look the other way—while also risking the re-authorization of law's authoritative institutions by working through them to win papers or amnesty for those who are here; then the poor migrants and refugees living in that murky space mentioned by Benhabib in the first lecture will not be so dependent on the law to position them with more clarity in its network. Then they will not have to wait for their time to come, and a good thing too—because it won't. For even when our time seems to have come, time can nonetheless still subject us to its trickery.

"This is a story about the trickery of time," is the first line of an article by Alex Kotlowitz about Ibrahim Parlak, a Kurd from Turkey and a would-be immigrant to the United States who was held for almost a year in detention and was almost deported to no-country as a result of the recasting of his past by post-9/11 politics and by likely abuses of discretionary power that post-dated his previously approved applications for asylum in the United States. Post hoc, Parlak was cast as a terrorist, but this has not yet erased from his neighbors' memories (not yet) his decade long membership in a Michigan community.[23] The activism of his many friends and supporters prevented him from becoming one of the disappeared, a casualty of policing and immigration policies that sprang up post 9/11 (but also pre 9/11: The Antiterrorism and Effective Death Penalty Act of 1996 played a role in his recasting, although again, due to time's trickery, even that legislation, a response to the Okalahoma City bombing, is now often assumed to be part of our post-9/11 landscape, in which the emergency is *foreign* terrorists, not domestic ones). A Federal Court ordered Parlak set free on bond on May 20, 2005. As this essay went to press, Parlak was preparing to appeal his deportation by the Department of Homeland Security's Immigration and Customs Enforcement Office, the Department of Homeland Security had appealed the federal court's decision to free Parlak on bail and lost, and was filing a motion to vacate the judge's order on a technicality.[24] Meanwhile a group called Free Ibrahim has formed. Their slogan is "Ibrahim for Citizen," and they have succeeded in getting Senator Carl Levin and two representatives to introduce two bills in the House and Senate to make Parlak a permanent resident should he fail to prevail in the courts.[25]

An agonistic cosmopolitics would approve of movements like this, and of those that demand alien suffrage for coresidents. But advocates of an agonistic cosmopolitics would work, at the same time, to prevent the energies of those movements from being lost once their state-centered and state-affirming goals are won. Or we might declare our cities to be sister cities in solidarity with cities from other nation states, thus inaugurating all sorts of extrastatist relief, aid, trade, and learning between us.[26] Or we might see more citizens of privileged nations marrying, instrumentally, those who seek to live among them, in order thereby to enable their fellow world-dwellers to stay on as their neighbors and, as a nice by-product, thereby deromanticizing *two* institutions insistently romanticized and still claimed by most states as their monopoly, both marriage and citizenship.[27] Practices such as these and others are designated by Etienne Balibar, who draws on Bodin, as "marks of sovereignty," in a move meant to take Bodin and democratic sovereignty back from the state sovereigntists.[28] Such practices are jurisgenerative in Robert Cover's sense perhaps more than in Benhabib's because, although she does not mention it, the jurisgenerative in Cover's account is always partnered with the jurispathic. Generativity without destruction is no more possible for Cover than is hospitality without hostility for Derrida.

Were all this to happen and to be visible to us (for it does happen, but it is often not visible) through lenses that do not *privilege* (although they do take note of and seek to engage, improve, and democratize) formal legal, state, state-like, and interstate institutions, then we might see more worldliness, in Hannah Arendt's sense of care for the world. For, contra Benhabib, Arendt is no "Kantian when it comes to morals." Arendt's Kant is that of the Third Critique, not the Second. Moreover, Arendt is not, nor are postmodernists (so-called) "skeptical about putting the political under the moral," as Benhabib put it on the occasion of these lectures. Arendt has a critique of that.[29] Arendt did have a juridical moment in relation to Eichmann; who wouldn't? And, as Benhabib rightly points out, there is in Arendt a persistent (even naïve) legalism that is on display in her *Eichmann in Jerusalem*. But the limits of that trait in Arendt's thinking are also on display in *Eichmann*, perhaps most especially so when Arendt derisively dismisses the survivor, K-Zetnik, for his inability to testify coherently before the Israeli court. In Arendt's cutting portrayal of this man's failure, the ruthlessness of her legalism is as apparent as its tone deafness, its inalertness to context.[30]

For Arendt, the chief political virtues are worldliness and care for the world; these trump her legalism, and they are in danger of being marginalized and sidelined, in my view, by the version of cosmopolitanism on offer here, in which law, states, and state-like and interstate institutions are our principal addressees (in all of Benhabib's examples), our guardians, ventriloquizers, impersonators, shapers and censors of our voice, our desires, our aspirations, our solidarities. Under the sign of worldliness, however, the many commonalities between a normative cosmopolitanism like Benhabib's and an agonistic cosmopolitics such as that outlined here are visible. Both are united by a common motivation and a common cause: to work through the paradoxes of politics in order to combat the abundant forces of inequality in our world and generate new sites of action in concert on behalf of worlds not yet built.

Notes

For discussions of the issues raised in this comment, I am indebted to Bruce Robbins, Linda Zerilli, Jill Frank, Patchen Markell, Wendy Brown, Bill Connolly, Judith Butler, Etienne Balibar, and Seyla Benhabib. Laura Ephraim provided valuable research assistance and help with manuscript preparation. Thanks are due as well to the Tanner Committee for asking me to serve as discussant on these lectures.

1. This raises the question, which I will not pursue, of the rhetorical function of Benhabib opening her reflections on transnationalism and multiculturalism with a rumination on Eichmann. The lens and mood set by Eichmann and genocide set us up to relate in a certain way—in a mode of dependence and felt need of rescue—to the project of interstate law and cosmopolitan norms. It is problematic in a way that recalls the question posed to Mike Dukakis in the 1988 American presidential election campaign, (something like) "what would you want done to the perpetrator, if your wife was raped and murdered?" One is thrust by the specters of genocide, rape and murder, into extremes of (il)legality.

2. Also not insignificant is this prohibition's linking of genocide with crimes against humanity. It thereby renders moot or in any case bypasses Arendt's abundant objections to the former (genocide) and her preference for the latter (crimes against humanity) as the proper name for crimes such as those we have since come to call "ethnic cleansing."

3. Arendt did, Benhabib acknowledges, write in the Postscript to *Eichmann in Jerusalem* that it "is inconceivable . . . that [an international] court would be a criminal tribunal which pronounces on the guilt or innocence of individuals" (1963, 298, quoted at 15), but Benhabib pronounces this statement "baffling" and explains that it is symptomatic of Arendt's "civic republican vision of political determination" (15), a vision in need of mediation or overcoming. Benhabib's lectures, positioned as they are as an effort to mediate between cosmopolitan norms and republican self-determination in part by way of practices of democratic iteration, might well be seen as Benhabib's own iterative effort to offer Arendt the middle way she did not see (or might have refused. But which is it?).

4. I discuss this in more detail in *Future Perfect* (unpublished manuscript).

5. Cosmopolitics is the term under which Pheng Cheah and Bruce Robbins gather a collection of essays exploring themes of hospitality,

transnational debt, and international engagement (*Cosmopolitics: Thinking and Feeling Beyond the Nation* [Minneapolis: University of Minnesota Press, 1998]). Notably, however, in his reading of Levinas, Derrida identifies Kant with a mere *cosmopolitics* and notes that Levinas never used that term, nor the more usual *cosmopolitanism*, preferring instead: *universalism*. Derrida suggests that Levinas abjured the term cosmopolitanism or cosmopolitics (Derrida does not here distinguish the two) for two reasons: "first, because this sort of political thought refers pure hospitality and this peace to an indefinite progress [which also always "retains the trace of a natural hostility" which is its point of departure in Kant]; second, because of the well-known ideological connotations with which modern anti-Semitism saddled the great tradition of a cosmopolitanism passed down from Stoicism or Pauline Christianity to the Enlightenment and to Kant" (*Adieu to Emmanuel Levinas* [Stanford: Stanford University Press, 1999], 88 [hereafter *Adieu*]).

6. *Rogues: Two Essays on Reason* (Stanford: Stanford University Press, 2005), 173 n. 12, citing *Of Hospitality* (Stanford: Stanford University Press, 2000), *On Cosmopolitanism and Forgiveness* (New York: Routledge, 2001), and *Adieu*.

7. This is reminiscent of Rogers Smith's effort to identify ascriptive moments in U.S. history not with the liberal tradition but with alternative, ascriptive rivals to that tradition (Rogers M. Smith, "Beyond Tocqueville, Myrdal, and Hartz: The Multiple Traditions in America," *American Political Science Review*, Vol. 87, No. 3 [Sept. 1993], pp. 549—566). On Smith, see Jacqueline Stevens, "Beyond Tocqueville, Please!," (published with a response from Smith in) *American Political Science Review*, Vol. 89, No. 4 (Dec. 1995), pp. 987—995 and my *Democracy and the Foreigner* (Princeton, N.J.: Princeton University Press, 2003), chaps. 1 and 5.

8. A similar point is made by Etienne Balibar, who says that Arendt's "'right to have rights' does not feature a *minimal* remainder of the political, made of juridical and moral claims to be protected by a constitution; it is much more the idea of a *maximum*. Or, better said, it refers to the continuous process in which a minimal recognition of the belonging of human beings to the 'common' sphere of existence (and therefore also work, culture, public and private speech) *already* involves—and makes possible—a totality of rights. I call this the 'insurrectional' element of democracy, which plays a determinant role in every constitution of a democratic or

republican state." *We, the People of Europe?* (Princeton, N.J.: Princeton University Press, 2003), p. 120. Note that democracy, quite properly, is not here cast as insurrectional but as having an "insurrectional element."

9. Indeed, Benhabib herself confesses in the final version of the lectures that she may have been, with regard to the French headscarf case, overly optimistic, given events in the year since. Etienne Balibar, by contrast, is not less optimistic. He is cutting: the Maastricht definition of European citizenship that awards EU citizenship to nationals of any constituent national state, he says, "immediately transforms a project of inclusion into a program of exclusion," given the size of the resident alien population in Europe at the time and given the dependence of Europe on that population's labor. *We, the People of Europe?* p. 122.

10. Balibar, *We, the People of Europe?* pp. 122, 162, and passim. For example, "European citizenship, within the limits of the currently existing union, is not conceived of as a recognition of the rights and contributions of *all* the communities present upon European soil, but as a postcolonial isolation of 'native' and 'nonnative' populations" (170).

11. I am thinking here of Arendt's discussion of the Dreyfus case as well as of her argument in *Origins of Totalitarianism* that police powers developed to deal with the stateless after World War II would, if left unchecked, soon be used against the general population (vol. I, chap. 4 and vol. II, chap. 9).

12. In her discussion of the French Mariannes, Benhabib leaves the terrain of law altogether to mark out the importance of cultural politics, with which I agree. In only one instance does Benhabib leave the terrain staked out by the binary of formal law versus democratic contestation to acknowledge the abundant powers of administrative discretion, and the example she mentions is a positive one of discretionary power used to the good: "Although officially the wearing of the 'turban' (a form of headscarf worn by observant Muslim women) is banned [in Turkey], many faculty members as well as administrators tolerate it when they can" (79). On discretion and the rule of law, see my "Bound by Law?" in *The Limits of Law*, ed. Sarat, Douglas, and Umphrey (Stanford University Press, 2005).

13. Here she seems almost to echo Julia Kristeva, whose (more) French universalism I criticized in detail in *Democracy and the Foreigner*, chap. 3.

14. In Canada, alien suffrage was ended at the same time as some women, (military wives), were first given the vote (1917—1918). Until then, coresidents were assumed to share a fate, a shared future, if not

a past. This is different from the German court's invocation of "fate" in its decision on alien suffrage, in which, it seems, the fact that people moved once (in a cross-border migration; presumably other residents had moved too but not across national borders), was taken as license to script those people as always about to leave. (This, it seems to me is the real offense, insofar as it bespeaks the unimaginability of real immigration. They may have come here but they are never really here because, having come from elsewhere, they will certainly leave; they will be called home? Or expelled, deported?)

15. At the lectures, Benhabib responded, as Habermas also has to objections like this one, by acknowledging the fact of the regress, saying, in effect, "Okay, one step forward two steps back." This response is different from the double gesture called for here insofar as it rescues progress from any evidence against it, and preserves the linearity of its timeline: progress and regress are two sides of the same coin and regress is here suffered due to the promise of progress. Thus, the alternative to progressive time is not regress but rather plural temporalities, an idea developed by William Connolly in his recent work, *Pluralism* (Duke University Press, 2005), and commented on by me in "The Time of Rights: Emergent Thoughts in an Emergency Setting," in *The New Pluralism*, edited by David Campbell and Morton Schoolman (Duke University Press, forthcoming).

16. The same might be said as well for the new human rights regime itself, which, as Derrida points out, is a new site of sovereignty and counters sovereignty with sovereignty, not with nonsovereignty.

17. Nevzat Soguk, *States and Strangers: Refugees and Displacements of Statecraft* (Minneapolis: University of Minnesota Press, 1990). On the camps, see Etienne Balibar, "Europe as Borderland," The Alexander von Humboldt Lecture in Human Geography, University of Nijmegen, November 10, 2004 and http://www.ru.nl/socgeo/n/colloquium/Europe%20as%20Borderland.pdf.

18. Giorgio Agamben, *Homo Sacer: Sovereign Power and Bare Life* (Stanford: Stanford University Press, 1998). I develop a critique of Agamben's overy capacious concepts of biopower and bare life in *Future Perfect*.

19. Here, Benhabib provides a minor amendment to Habermas, who treats constitutionalism as if it were merely the rule of law. He does not attend to constitutions as expressions of particularity. (I, myself, criticize

him on this point, as does Alessandro Ferrara. See our replies to Habermas: "Dead Rights, Live Futures," and "On Boats and Principles: Reflections on Habermas's 'Constitutional Democracy,'" *Political Theory* 29 [December 2001]: 782–791). Benhabib, by contrast, does emphasize the character of the act of political self-legislation as an act of self-constitution in which the 'we' defines itself as a 'we' in relation to a territorialized setting.

20. It is also hard to tell what's "iterative" about them. The term, in the hands of Derrida, whom Benhabib cites here, signifies a drift and residue, a ruptural quality of language, as such; hence "iteratibility" (not iteration) is his term, connoting something quite different from the subject-centered practice suggested here by the term "democratic iterations." Derrida meant to call attention by way of iterability to a quality of language and practice that pushes terms and concepts always to exceed and undo the intentions and aims of any particular speaker in time; this would include the languages of law and even universality itself (*Of Hospitality*, 65).

21. Most of the arguments relevant here are well summarized by Anand Bertrand Commissiong in the review of David Held, *Global Covenant: The Social Democratic Alternative to the Washington Consensus*, published in *Logos*, May 2005. "The challenges the authority and execution of international legal regimes face in controlling these [i.e., anti modern] forces [both of Bush's messianism and of Islamic extremists] illustrate further the complexities of the stalemate. As Tocqueville noted, courts in a democracy represent an un-democratic strain essential to the system's proper functioning. The relation between natural law and democratic will, a key component of modernity, was accomplished over several hundred years partly through the compromise of political negotiation in successful national formation processes in Europe and North America. But this process in many cases also violently ruled out effectively dissolutionary elements that sought to establish smaller, autonomous units. (Tilly) Even in some Western countries these forces were not entirely pacified and still simmer ... [Held's] vision can only be realized if some sense of world-wide solidarity, or covenant if you will, develops to take shared control of these networks."

22. Michael Rogin, *Ronald Reagan, the Movie, and Other Episodes in Political Demonology* (Berkeley: University of California Press, 1987).

23. "The Politics of Ibrahim Parlak: How did a political refugee who became a popular café owner in a small Michigan town suddenly become a

terrorist in the eyes of the government? A post 9/11 story," Alex Kotlowitz, *New York Times Magazine*, Mar. 20, 2005, p. 46.

24. U.S. District Judge Avern Cohn set bail at $50,000 for Parlak on May 21, 2005, deciding that he should be freed while he appeals his deportation. As the *Chicago Sun-Times* reported, Judge Cohn reasoned that otherwise Parlak "was likely to be held for an unreasonable time period, given the complexity of his deportation case." Released on bond on June 3, Parlak is back in Harbert, Michigan for the time being while his lawyers prepare his appeal. *Ibrahim Parlak v. Robin Baker* (Detroit Field Office Director, U.S. Immigration and Customs), U.S. District Court for the Eastern District of Michigan Case No. 05-70826. See also "Jailed Immigrant to Get out on Bond," by Monifa Thomas, *Chicago Sun-Times*, May 21, 2005, p. 6; and "Family, Friends Embrace Parlak," by Jeff Romig, *South Bend Tribune*, June 4, 2005, p. A1, and http://www.harborcountry-news.com/articles/2006/03/23/news/story2.txt.

25. See www.freeibrahim.com.

26. On sister cities, see chap. 3, *Democracy and the Foreigner* and the several sources cited therein. Derrida also looks to cities as a source of promise for a new cosmopolitanism: see *On Cosmopolitanism and Forgiveness*.

27. Entry into citizenship and entry into marriage, at least normalized, permitted marriage, are two of those moments (paradoxically permanent moments) at which the state's role as authorizer empowers it over those who seek its recognition and rewards. States, the United States in particular, insist that we treat both institutions romantically, not instrumentally. Both are contracts that we must enter into with the least contractual motives, out of a noninstrumental desire to belong, or to share, or to contribute but never out of a desire to profit in any way from the relationship. This indeed is the quandary faced by those who seek refuge in states such as France and the United States. Neediness marks the would-be immigrant as an undesirable. But, as Etienne Balibar points out in *We, the People of Europe?* who but the needy would come? I discuss the connections between marriage and citizenship in "Foreign Brides, Family Ties, and New World Masculinity," in chapter 4 of *Democracy and the Foreigner*.

28. Balibar calls also for works of citizenship that engage economic power or religious knowledge in comparative perspective, in "Difficult Europe," in *We, the People of Europe*, p. 173 and passim.

29. For an analysis of Arendt's critique of moralized politics and of the Kantian injunction that politics should bend its knee to morality, see my *Political Theory and the Displacement of Politics* (Ithaca, N.Y.: Cornell University Press, 1993), chap. 4.

30. *Eichmann in Jerusalem*, 223–224. For an alternative, more empathic and insightful treatment of the K-Zetnick episode, see Shoshana Felman, *The Juridical Unconscious: Trials and Traumas of the Twentieth Century* (Cambridge, Mass.: Harvard University Press, 2002).

Liberal Nationalism and Cosmopolitan Justice

WILL KYMLICKA

Seyla Benhabib's lecture discusses a number of important developments in Europe, developments that challenge our most basic ideas of the nature of political community and of membership within it. I have a different interpretation of some of these developments and of their implications for political philosophy, which I will try to spell out in this short commentary. Before getting to the specifics, however, let me step back and try to situate the debate.

National and Postnational Citizenship

Within recent Anglo-American political philosophy, the predominant ideal of political community and of citizenship has two main features. The first concerns underlying values, which have typically been defined in *liberal-democratic* terms. If citizenship can be understood in part as a package of rights and responsibilities, then this package has been defined by reference to liberal-democratic values. At the heart of our citizenship rights are individual liberties. These include freedom of association, speech and conscience, and more generally freedom of choice about how to lead our lives. Similarly, our duties as citizens are quintessentially liberal duties—for example, the duty to be tolerant, to accept the secular nature of political power and hence the separation of church and state, to exercise our individual autonomous judgement when engaging in voting or public reasoning.

The second feature concerns the boundaries of citizenship, which have invariably been defined in *national* terms. If citizenship can be understood in part as membership in a political community, then the traditional model of citizenship emphasizes membership in national political communities. The nation-state has been seen as the privileged locus for political participation, self-government, and solidarity. If democracy is the rule "of the people," then it is the nation that defines "the people" who are to rule themselves. We exercise self-determination through electing national legislatures, and our citizenship rights are protected by national constitutions.

This model of citizenship based on liberal-democratic values institutionalized in national political communities is relatively recent. Very few political communities were either liberal-democratic in orientation or national in scope two hundred years ago. Yet we have witnessed two overwhelming trends in the last two centuries in the West: (1) the nearly-universal reordering of political space from a confusing welter of empires, kingdoms, city-states, protectorates, and colonies into a system of nation-states, all of which have embarked on "nation-building" policies aimed at the diffusion of a common national identity, culture, and language throughout the territory of the state; and (2) the nearly universal replacement of all forms of preliberal or nondemocratic forms of government (e.g., monarchies, oligarchies, theocracies, fascist regimes, military dictatorships, Communist regimes, etc.) with systems of liberal-democracy.

Let's call this the model of "liberal nationhood." In my view, it has been a remarkable success in ensuring democracy, individual rights, peace and security, and economic prosperity for an ever-increasing number of people. It has provided the basis for the emergence of what Dominique Schnapper calls the "providential state," in which state institutions have the capacity and intention to improve the well-being of their citizens.[1]

However, these successes have been achieved at a high cost. Building liberal-democracy on national foundations has historically involved a number of injustices against those who are not seen as full members of the nation, whether they are inside the boundaries of the state or outside. Victims of liberal nationhood include (1) immigrants, who have typically faced exclusion or assimilation at the hands of liberal nation-states; (2) historic substate groups, such as indigenous peoples or regional minorities, whose distinct national identity and aspirations to national autonomy have typically been suppressed by liberal nation-states;[2] and (3) neighboring nation-states, because national identities are often defined precisely by antagonism to neighboring nations, creating the potential for interstate rivalries and hostilities.[3] In each case, people who do not belong to the privileged national group are seen as threats to be contained or suppressed.

Defenders of liberal nationhood say that these harms are not intrinsic to the model but, rather, are perversions of it. These harms reflect illiberal rather than liberal forms of nationalism, and/or reflect chauvinism or imperialism rather than nationalism per se. What distinguishes liberal from illiberal nationhood, it is argued, is a tolerance of diversity; and what distinguishes nationalism from chauvinism is a willingness to extend the same rights to other nations that one claims for oneself, whether these are substate "nations within" or neighboring nation-states.[4]

Yet it is undeniable that these harms are inherent risks of the pursuit of liberal nationhood, and indeed have been responsible for some of the gravest injustices of the twentieth century. Faced with this dilemma, there are two broad options. One is to preserve the basic framework of liberal nationhood, but to try to reduce these risks by, for example, (1) adopting a more "multicultural" conception of nationhood to accommodate immigrants; (2) adopting a "multi-nation" conception of the state that recognizes the existence of substate nations and indigenous peoples, and accords them a significant degree of national autonomy; and (3) adopting geopolitical security arrangements that inhibit aggression between nation-states. We can see movement in the West in all of these directions, in an attempt to preserve the benefits of liberal nationhood while reducing its risks. Let's call this the "taming liberal nationhood" approach.

The second option is to try to build new forms of "postnational" or "cosmopolitan" citizenship that sever the link between liberal-democracy and nationhood, and thereby entirely avoid the risks of liberal nationalism. Let's call this the "transcending liberal nation-hood" approach.

There's a growing debate in political philosophy about these two options. In North America, the debate remains a highly speculative one, but in Europe it is not just a philosophical debate. It is also a press-ing political issue, due to various forms of "Europeanization," includ-ing the European Union, the European Court of Human Rights, the Parliamentary Assembly of the Council of Europe, and so on. These new supranational legal and political institutions provide an infra-structure that can be deployed for either taming or transcending lib-eral nationhood. As a result, these two options are a matter of serious political contestation, not just philosophical debate.

In her lectures, Benhabib focuses on several developments in Europe that she suggests are instantiations of the second, transcend-ing, option. She says that developments regarding immigrants in France and Germany have repudiated the "vanishing ideology of nationhood" (65), in part because they involve the "disaggregating" of rights from national citizenship. As I understand her, she wants to claim not only that these processes of transcending liberal nation-hood are occurring empirically, but that they should be normatively endorsed and promoted.

My own view is different, on both the descriptive and normative levels. Empirically, I believe that developments in Europe are better understood as instantiations of the first model. They are serving to tame not transcend liberal nationhood. Indeed, they are intended not only to help tame liberal nationhood where it already exists, but also to help diffuse the model of a (tamed) liberal nationhood to countries where it does not yet exist. Far from challenging the "vanishing ideol-ogy" of nationhood, European institutions are spreading it. They are remaking Europe in the image of (or according to the ideology of) lib-eral nationhood. This is internationalization in the service of liberal nationhood. I think this is true in general about the processes of European integration, and also about the specific cases that Benhabib discusses.

I also differ with her on the normative issues. The fact that European integration is taming rather than transcending liberal nationhood is not a cause for moral regret. On the contrary, the development of pan-European institutions and organizations is morally progressive even if their function is limited to the taming and diffusing of liberal nationhood. Indeed, I would argue that Europeanization is morally progressive *because* it is consolidating and diffusing liberal nationhood. That is a morally progressive project, worthy of our support, which has already brought political benefits of great value to the people of Europe.

These are the areas of possible disagreements that I will explore in my comments. I say "possible" disagreement, because I'm not entirely sure that Benhabib really does want to transcend liberal nationhood. Part of her aim in the lectures is to illustrate the dynamics of "democratic iterations," and in particular the fact that:

Rights and other principles of the liberal-democratic state need to be periodically challenged and rearticulated in the public sphere in order to retain and enrich their original meaning. It is only when new groups claim that they belong within the circles of addressees of a right from which they have been excluded in its initial articulation that we come to understand the fundamental limitedness of every rights claim within a constitutional tradition as well as its context-transcending validity. (60)

I fully agree with this sentiment, as well as her concluding claim that "jurisgenerative politics" in Europe is increasing "the threshold of justification to which formerly exclusionary practices are now submitted. Exclusions take place, but the threshold for justifying them is now higher" (71).

One possible reading of these passages is precisely as manifestations of the "taming" strategy. Democratic iterations and jurisgenerative politics relating to immigrants in Europe presuppose the model of liberal nationhood but seek to reduce the risks of exclusion that accompany it. If this is her view, then there may be very little dis-agreement between us. Other passages in the lectures, however, sug-gest that she views the new claims being advanced in these democratic iterations as repudiating or transcending the ideology of liberal nationhood. If so, our disagreement may be more substantial.

My goal in these comments, therefore, is to push Benhabib to clar-ify the link between democratic iterations regarding cosmopolitan norms and liberal nationhood. Like Benhabib, I strongly support the European Court of Human Rights and the International Criminal Court, and I share her view that everyone who is affected by these cosmopolitan norms must be able to participate in deliberations about them. My only point of potential disagreement concerns the link between cosmopolitan norms and liberal nationhood. As against those who see cosmopolitanism and liberal nationhood as inherent-ly in tension, I want to argue that one conception of the nature and function of cosmopolitan norms is precisely to promote (a tamed form of) liberal nationhood, and that this conception is conceptually coherent, politically feasible, and morally progressive.

The Case of the EU

The two main cases that Benhabib discusses regarding immigrants in France and Germany are complex, and I will return to them later. However, the more general issues at stake in the choice between tam-ing and transcending liberal nationhood are perhaps clearer in the case of the EU itself. Some commentators (and actors) view the EU as a vehicle for transcending liberal nationhood. For these "transcen-ders," the world-historical task of the EU is to develop a non-nation-al or postnational view of citizenship and of the demos.

This development has typically involved two distinct issues: insti-tutions and identities. Institutionally, transcenders argue that the political status of persons in the EU should no longer be mediated by national citizenship, and that popular sovereignty should no longer be primarily embodied in national legislatures. Viewed this way, it is a defect of the EU as currently structured that (a) European citizenship still remains derivative of national citizenship, and (b) the (directly elected) European Parliament remains subservient to the (nationally delegated) European Commission. These are defects because they fail to satisfactorily sever the link between liberal-democratic citizenship and nationhood.

This project of institutional reform is typically tied to a project of changing people's identities so as to displace the privileged position of national identities. For transcenders, it is a problem when most people continue to identify themselves in Eurobarometer surveys primarily in terms of national identity, and a sign of moral progress whenever these surveys show increases in the number of people who say they feel "more European than German" (or "equally European as German"). For transcenders, we need more proactive attempts to promote a European identity through education and cultural exchanges (such as the enormous Erasmus program of university exchanges).

On both the institutional and identity dimensions, the EU is viewed by most transcenders as a series of lost opportunities, because it has (so far) failed to displace national citizenship, national legislatures and national identities as the main locus of political energies. For transcenders, politics in Europe remains too "nation-centric," and the moral value of the EU depends on changing this.

For the "tamers," by contrast, the world-historical task of the EU is to tame and diffuse liberal nationhood, and in this respect it has arguably been a spectacular success. It has "tamed" liberal nationhood by reducing the risk of war between Western democracies (particularly France and Germany); and also by providing a safe umbrella for the domestic accommodation of substate nations (e.g., in Catalonia; Flanders; South Tyrol; Northern Ireland).[5] Even more important, it has helped diffuse the model of liberal nationhood, first to southern Europe (e.g., Spain, Portugal; Greece), and more recently to central and eastern Europe (e.g., Poland; Hungary; Slovakia; Slovenia;

Czech Republic). The EU has enabled former fascist and Communist countries to become "normal" liberal nation-states (or multination federations), and to enjoy the benefits of a normal liberal national political life. Far from transcending liberal nationhood, the EU is universalizing it, reordering Europe in its image.

In my view, this is an enormous moral achievement, dwarfing in significance any alleged benefits from, say, the strengthening of the European Parliament, or the inculcation of feelings of "being European."[6] The failure to recognize this moral achievement is, I think, a moral blindness of the political theory literature on the EU.[7]

This debate between tamers and transcenders has important political consequences, particularly regarding the choice between "widening" and "deepening" the EU. Many transcenders wanted to delay the expansion of the EU, because including new countries would make it more difficult to build up feelings of familiarity, trust and solidarity within the EU, and also make it more difficult for pan-European deliberations to take place, either at the level of civil society or the European parliament. Including large numbers of former communist countries, or even Muslim countries, would weaken the sense that citizens of the EU share common experiences and common values, and make it more likely that the EU would remain primarily a club of states pursuing their mutual advantage, rather than a truly new form of post-national demos. It was better, they argued, to "deepen" the EU before "widening" it.[8]

By contrast, for the tamers, the choice between deepening and widening the EU is a no-brainer. Since the main task of the EU to tame and diffuse liberal nationhood, it should expand as quickly as possible, as widely as possible. The peoples of southeastern Europe and the former Soviet Union are very unlikely to enjoy the benefits of a peaceful liberal-democratic national political life without the incentives, pressures and resources of the EU. Many of these states are weak and divided, living in rough neighbourhoods, and their hope for a normal national political life depends on the expansion of the EU. If the EU can do for Macedonia or Turkey what it did for Spain—that is, enable them to become normal, democratic multination federations—that would be a great moral accomplishment. By comparison, any moral benefit from deepening the EU is, in my view, minimal.

The Case of Immigrants in France and Germany

All of this may seem off-topic, as Benhabib's main focus is on the case of immigrants in Europe. I've argued that we can view European integration as a vehicle for taming and diffusing liberal nationhood; that this is a morally progressive project, and moreover that it has been a considerable success, particularly with respect to two of the main risks of liberal nationhood: ensuring peaceful relations across state borders and accommodating substate nations within borders. But Benhabib's focus is on the needs of immigrants in Europe, particularly in Germany and France, who have been subject to either exclusion or assimilation under traditional models of liberal nationhood. Could it be that in this case we need to transcend, and not just tame, liberal nationhood?

It is true that, in contrast to the two areas I have just discussed, the EU has not been a particularly progressive force on issues of immigration. In the process of taming and diffusing liberal nationhood, it has not yet forcefully challenged exclusionary or assimilationist conceptions of immigrant integration. Like Benhabib, I think that cosmopolitan norms can and should be developed to contest these conceptions.

But what should the content of these cosmopolitan norms be? Here again, we face a choice between taming and transcending liberal nationhood. As I suggested earlier, the taming model would involve shifting toward a more "multicultural" conception of liberal nationhood. This shift has already taken place in several Western democracies, such as Australia, Canada, the United States, and Britain. Its basic outlines include (a) relatively easy access to citizenship after, say, three to five years of residency, with minimal tests of national integration, including knowledge of the national language, knowledge of national history and institutions, and an oath of loyalty to the country and its constitution; (b) reasonable accommodation of immigrant ethnicity within public institutions, such as changes to dress codes, public holidays, multicultural school curricula; and so on. There are by now well-developed theories and practices of accommodating immigrant multiculturalism as part of a (tamed) liberal nationhood.[9]

So far as I can tell, the developments that Benhabib discusses in France and Germany are all consistent with this basic model for taming liberal nationalism through a multicultural conception of nationhood. The "democratic iterations" that she describes, and the "jurisgenerative politics" that she endorses, all seem consistent with this basic model.

Benhabib herself, however, implies that these democratic iterations are pushing beyond the limits of liberal nationhood. According to Benhabib, the liberal nationhood approach involves two links: first, the rights of immigrants are linked to the acquisition of citizenship; and second, the acquisition of citizenship is tied up with "national integration." She focuses on three claims made by immigrants in Europe that she believes are challenging these links, and hence transcending liberal nationhood:

1. claims regarding the rights of noncitizens, including local voting rights;
2. claims about the rules for naturalization of immigrants; and
3. claims about accommodating religious practices, particularly the wearing of the headscarf.

She suggests that all three of these claims involve some departure from the "vanishing ideology of nationhood," either by unbundling rights from formal citizenship or by unbundling citizenship from nationhood.

I think this is misleading.[10] To explain why, recall the situation of the Turks in Germany, whose claims are at the heart of Benhabib's examples. They were originally admitted as "guest-workers" on temporary work visas. As such, they were ineligible for citizenship and were denied many of the rights possessed by German citizens, including various civil, social and economic rights as well as political rights, on the expectation they would return home. It soon became clear, however, that the Turks were not voluntarily returning, and so a decision had to be made about their legal status.

To oversimplify, there were four options:

1. deny all social, economic and political rights to the Turks, in order to make their status in Germany insecure and unpleasant, so that they would return home;
2. unbundle some rights from citizenship in the hope that their status would then be tolerable, so that they wouldn't demand full citizenship. On this view, unbundled rights are an alternative to national citizenship;
3. unbundle some rights from citizenship in the hope that this would promote the integration of Turks into German society, reduce prejudice, build loyalty, and hence lead eventually to acceptance of full citizenship. On this view, unbundled rights are seen as "proto-citizen" rights, as a transition to national citizenship; or
4. make all permanent residents immediately eligible for naturalization, and hence eligible for the full bundle of citizenship rights.

In general, the right in Germany endorsed the first two options, whereas the left endorsed the latter two options. [11]

This is a very schematic account of the debate in Germany, but it should immediately be clear that the idea of unbundling rights from citizenship is not, in and of itself, a politically progressive position. For many on the right in Germany, it was a tool for avoiding the granting of full and equal citizenship. And, for that reason, many members of the left were hesitant about accepting the unbundling of rights from citizenship, unless they could be sure that it would not serve as a tool for continued exclusion. Hence, they demanded that any unbundling of rights be simultaneously accompanied by liberalization of naturalization. On this view, the unbundling of rights from citizenship is legitimate as a transitional phase towards full national citizenship—that is, the long-term goal must be the "rebundling" of rights and citizenship. Temporary unbundling is politically progressive if and when it serves as a step towards rebundling in the form of full and equal citizenship within the framework of liberal nationhood.

We can see the same debate between left and right regarding local voting rights. For some on the right, granting immigrants local voting rights was a way of defusing demands for national citizenship. A more complex version of this view suggested that if immigrants could have both local citizenship and European citizenship, it would not be necessary to grant them access to German citizenship. Turks would be citizens of Berlin and citizens of Europe, but not citizens of Germany, thereby conveniently sparing Germans the effort of having to adopt a more racially and religiously inclusive conception of their nation. Surprisingly, some people on the left accepted this as a viable and progressive solution, primarily because it seemed to break the link between citizenship and nationhood. Since this approach disconnected both local and European citizenship from nationhood, it was seen as dealing a double-blow to the obsolete ideology of nationhood. Yet in reality, this was a politically regressive appeasement of conservative nationalism, and it is increasingly recognized as such within the German left. A politically progressive defense of local voting rights for aliens must view it as a proto-citizenship right; that is, as a form of political socialization into the national political system, enabling immigrants to develop bonds of trust and attachment towards national institutions, and hence as a step towards full national citizenship.[12]

So the idea of unbundling rights from citizenship—whether social rights or local voting rights—has served competing political projects in the European context, some regressive and some progressive. The regressive version views unbundling as an alternative to a more multicultural conception of liberal nationhood, whereas the progressive version views it as a step towards that goal. For a brief period of time, there were some people on the left in Germany who toyed with the idea that unbundling rights could be a progressive alternative to liberal nationhood, but that view has been largely repudiated, and there is a growing consensus on the left across Europe that any progressive version of the unbundling strategy has to be tied to the long-term goal of full national citizenship.[13]

This raises the second link mentioned earlier—namely, the link between formal state citizenship and "nationhood." Even if we agree that being a citizen of Berlin and Europe is not an acceptable alternative to being a citizen of Germany, in what sense is German (or French) citizenship linked to ideologies of nationhood?

This leads us to Benhabib's discussion of Muslims and headscarves. There is no question that many Western countries, including France and Germany, have historically had a conception of "national identity" and national integration that is inhospitable to Muslims, and other nonwhite or non-Christian minorities. This has sometimes been reflected in exclusionary or assimilationist naturalization rules (e.g., the old German requirement that immigrants "renounce exaggerated national-religious behavior")[14], and sometimes in more general rules about civic behavior (as in the current French debate about wearing the headscarf in school).

Do we need to renounce the link between citizenship and nationhood in order to contest these exclusions? In order to accommodate the legitimate claims of Muslim immigrants in Germany or France, do we need to reject the principle that the acquisition and exercise of state citizenship should be tied to some idea of integration into a German or French nation?

Benhabib suggests so, but I would argue that we already have ample evidence from other countries (including the United States and Canada) that "thinner" models of national identity can evolve that accommodate the transnational loyalties and religious identities of immigrants, including Muslim immigrants. The idea that models of liberal nationhood need to be transcended in order to fairly accommodate Muslims seems demonstrably refuted by the experience of the traditional countries of immigration. They have not had to abandon liberal nationhood in order to facilitate the naturalization of immigrants, or to allow Muslim girls to wear headscarves. The claims made by immigrants in France and Germany that Benhabib interprets as challenging liberal nationhood are well within the boundaries of what other liberal nations have already achieved in terms of developing more inclusive models of nationhood.[15] These countries have developed models of multicultural nationhood that are still very much national in ideology, diffused by a wide range of familiar nation-building policies, yet inclusive of religious and racial diversity, and accommodating of ethnic and religious practices.[16]

And it is precisely toward such liberal models of national identity that many Muslim groups in France are appealing. When asserting their right to wear a headscarf, they are not saying that they have this right as "Europeans," or as "Parisians," but precisely *as French citizens*. They argue that being Muslim is one way of being French, and that the right to appear in public as a Muslim is one of the rights guaranteed by the French constitution, and indeed is one of the rights that France bequeathed to the world. And of course they make these arguments in French, to their French conationals. This is the very paradigm of an argument that operates within the framework of liberal nationhood.

It is an interesting question why France and Germany (and other continental European countries) are so reluctant to accept these demands for a more multicultural conception of liberal nationhood.[17] At best, these countries are slouching toward this model, at worst they are moving away from it. But whatever the explanation, it remains the goal of democratic iterations by many Muslims in France and Germany, and I believe that it remains the only viable long-term solution.

In sum, then, I'm not sure that any of the three cases raised by Benhabib provide clear examples of a break with the ideology of liberal nationhood. The claims of immigrants in Europe with respect to aliens' rights, naturalization, and religious accommodation all fit comfortably within the conceptual framework of a multicultural conception of liberal-democratic/national citizenship, and all fall within the well-established practices of existing multicultural liberal nations. In this context, as more generally, the emerging cosmopolitan norms are serving to tame and diffuse liberal nationhood, not transcend it.

Notes

1. Schnapper, *La démocratie providentielle: Essai sur l'égalité contemporaine* (Paris: Gallimard, NRF Essais, 2002). In this context, we can recall Peter Ekeh's famous statement that the state in Africa is strong enough to harm its citizens, but too weak to help them. The existence of such "predatory" states, or merely weak and indifferent states, has been the norm historically.

2. The tendency for nation-states to suppress substate national groups in the name of nation-building is nicely captured in Walker Connor's influential article "Nation-Building or Nation-Destroying?" *World Politics*, Vol. 24 (1972): 319–355.

3. See Nenad Miscevic, "Close Strangers: Nationalism, Proximity and Cosmopolitanism," *Studies in East European Thought*, Vol. 88/11 (1999): 109–125. Miscevic argues that although a strong national identity is consistent with support for cosmopolitan norms, and with solidarity with distant peoples, it typically involves hostility toward neighboring nations.

4. Walzer calls this "the test of the next nation." Michael Walzer, "Nation and Universe," *Tanner Lectures on Human Values Vol XI*, ed. Grethe Peterson (Salt Lake City: University of Utah Press, 1990).

5. For the pivotal role of the EU in enabling these accommodations, see Michael Keating and John McGarry (eds.), *Minority Nationalism and the Changing International Order* (Oxford: Oxford University Press, 2001).

6. I say "alleged" benefit because there is some evidence that feelings of "being European" are in fact equated with greater xenophobia, not less. See Laurent Licata and Olivier Klein, "Does European Citizenship Breed Xenophobia: European Identification as a Predictor of Intolerance Towards Immigrants," *Journal of Community and Applied Social Psychology*, Vol. 12 (2002): 323–337.

7. Why is this moral achievement not recognized in much of the literature, even among those political theorists who are concerned with a moral
evaluation of the EU? Perhaps because, for transcenders, the diffusion of
liberal nationhood cannot count as moral progress. On the contrary, diffusing the "obsolete" ideology of nationhood is morally regressive. For
transcenders, the task of the EU is precisely to break the back of this ideology. Hence their blindness to one of its real moral achievements.

8. For a good overview of the "widening versus deepening debate," see
James Caporaso, *The European Union: Dilemmas of Regional Integration*
(Boulder, Colo.: Westview, 2000).

9. I try to develop my own model of multicultural liberal nationhood
that can accommodate immigrant ethnicity in *Politics in the Vernacular:
Nationalism, Multiculturalism, and Citizenship* (New York: Oxford
University Press, 2001). Other versions are developed in Joseph Carens,
Culture, Citizenship, and Community (Oxford: Oxford University Press,
2000); and Jeff Spinner, *The Boundaries of Citizenship* (Baltimore: Johns
Hopkins University Press, 1994).

10. It is widely agreed across the political spectrum that certain minimal
basic rights do not depend on citizenship. These include basic civil rights
(e.g., to free speech, association, worship), as well as basic humanitarian
rights (e.g., to health care; education). These are disconnected, not only
from national citizenship but also from permanent residency status. They
must be provided, not only to permanent residents but also to (e.g.) foreign students or temporary workers. The dispute about "unbundling"
rights from citizenship primarily concerns the more expansive set of
socio-economic rights and benefits—for example, to subsidized housing;
job training programs; university scholarships; eligibility for civil service
jobs—as well as local and national voting rights.

11. For a good overview of the partisan dimensions of this debate, see
Thomas Faist, "How to Define a Foreigner? The Symbolic Politics of
Immigration in German Partisan Discourse, 1978–1993," *West European
Politics*, Vol. 17/2: 50–71; Peter A. Kraus and Karen Schönwälder,
"Multiculturalism in Germany: Rhetoric, Scattered Experiments and
Future Chances," in Will Kymlicka and Keith Banting (eds.), *Multi-
culturalism and the Welfare State: Recognition and Redistribution in
Contemporary Democracies* (Oxford University Press, forthcoming).

12. In that sense, far from transcending liberal nationhood, the German debate about the rights of aliens is a paradigm case of the ineluctability of that model. On the enduring national dimensions to the evolution of aliens' rights, see Christian Joppke, "The Evolution of Alien Rights in the United States, Germany and the European Union," in A. Aleinikoff and D. Klusmeyer (eds.), *Citizenship Today: Global Perspectives and Practices* (Washington, D.C.: Carnegie Endowment for International Peace, 2001), 36–62.

13. I'm not sure whether Benhabib would disagree with any of this. Because she endorses the recent German reforms to facilitate access to national citizenship, she might well agree that unbundling rights from citizenship is not an acceptable alternative to (rebundled) national citizenship.

14. German Interior Ministry guidelines on naturalization, quoted in Sandra Schmidt, "Immigration Policy and new ethnic minorities in contemporary Germany," in Karl Cordell (ed.), *Ethnicity and Democratisation in the New Europe* (London: Routledge, 1999), pp. 91–105 at 103.

15. If our goal is to identify the outer limits of what liberal nationhood can accommodate, France and Germany are not good test cases. Many other Western liberal-democracies have gone farther in accommodating immigrants, both in terms of facilitated naturalization and cultural accommodation in public institutions.

16. In these countries, policies to accommodate immigrant ethnicity operate alongside policies to diffuse a common national language, national symbols and heroes, national holidays and toponyms, all with the intention of promoting a feeling of belonging to a single nation that belongs together in a common state, with a shared past and common future. In this sense, thinner notions of a "multicultural" nation are still very much notions of *nationhood*: citizens are still expected to speak a common national language, share a common national identity, feel loyalty to national institutions, and share a commitment to maintaining the nation as a single, self-governing community on its national territory into the indefinite future. For a more detailed account of how multiculturalism operates within the framework of liberal nation-building policies, see my *Politics in the Vernacular*.

17. For my speculations on this, see "Marketing Canadian Pluralism in the International Arena," *International Journal*, Vol. 59/4 (2004), pp. 829–852.

Reply to Commentators

Seyla Benhabib

Hospitality, Sovereignty, and Democratic Iterations

In "Cosmopolitan Norms," Jeremy Waldron observes that "there are already many norms in the world which operate at a cosmopolitan level, including (for example) the principles that define human rights and crimes against humanity, the laws that govern refuge, asylum, travel and migration, and the dense thicket of rules that sustain our life together, a life shared by people and peoples, not just in any particular society but generally on the face of the earth" (83). Waldron complains that philosophers and political theorists are not much interested in "the dense thicket of rules that sustain our life together," because "we don't like commerce (because we are largely ignorant of it), and we would prefer not to have to write about it" (84). In discussing the *status and emergence* of cosmopolitan norms, Waldron suggests that we should focus on quotidian norms at least as much as on high profile issues like *l'affaire du foulard*.

Put briefly, Waldron thinks that it is more appropriate to consider cosmopolitan norms along the model of *lex mercatoria*, rather than along the model of crimes against humanity, laws regulating refuge and asylum and the like. He accuses me of "state-centrism" on account of my principal focus upon the latter to the neglect of the former. Along the way, disagreements emerge about my reading of Kant's cosmopolitan right, about how legal norms arise in societies, and about the relationship of cosmopolitan norms and municipal (national) law. Jeremy Waldron's interesting comments do not so much *resolve* the issues raised in my Tanner Lectures but, rather, they *dissolve* them in an ordinary language, neo-Wittgensteinian

approach to philosophical arguments. Furthermore, his view of commerce reminds me of nineteenth-century free-trade utopias in its
confidence that everyday trading practices would lead to the rise and
spread of cosmopolitan norms.

At the center of much of our disagreement is interpreting Kant's
doctrine of *jus cosmopoliticum,* which can be rendered into English
as "cosmopolitan right" or "cosmopolitan law." I read Kant's doctrine of universal hospitality as opening up a space of discourse, a
space of articulation, for "all human rights claims which are cross-
border in scope." Waldron thinks that this may be pushing the text
too far; but even granting me this interpretation, he is concerned that
there may be a conflation in my reading of Kant between what falls
under the scope of cosmopolitan right and what would fall under
"the right of nations" or *Voelkerrecht* (89).

Kant recognized three distinct though related levels of rightful relations as the basis of his tripartite division of the law. As Katrin
Flickschuh observes, "the 'Right of a State' (Staatenrecht) specifies
relations of Right between persons within a state; the 'Right of Nations'
(Voelkerrecht) pertains to relations of Right between states; and 'the
Right for all nations' or 'cosmopolitan Right' (Weltbuergerrecht)
concerns relations of Right between persons and foreign states."[1] The
originality of Kant's "Perpetual Peace" essay derives not only from his
doctrine of hospitality but also from the cumulative normative import
of all three definitive articles of perpetual peace read together. Kant
formulates three "definitive articles for perpetual peace among states."
These read: "The Civil Constitution of Every State should be
Republican;" "The Law of Nations shall be founded on a Federation of
Free States;" and "The Law of World Citizenship Shall be Limited to
Conditions of Universal Hospitality."[2] (Kant [1795] 1923, pp. 434–446;
[1795] 1994, pp. 99–108.) Each of these articles straddles the traditional
distinctions between municipal (national) law, "law of nations" and
"cosmopolitan law" in an interesting way. The first article of "Perpetual
Peace," which stipulates that the civil constitution of every state should
be republican, prescribes that all national legislation ought to respect

the *freedom* of individuals as humans by subjecting them to a common source of law; it should guarantee their *equality* as citizens through equal treatment in the eyes of the law; and it should safeguard their *independence* as civil subjects. Thus, this first article *articulates* a set of universal standards by which to judge a constitution if it is to be deemed legitimate, thereby piercing the shield of state sovereignty. Likewise, the second article of "Perpetual Peace" does not restrict the domain of law of nations to treaties governing war, peace, trade, and other transactions among peoples, but pushes the law of nations toward a model of constitutionalization, that is, toward the subjection of all sovereigns to a common source of law, irrespective of whether this federation takes the form of a treaty among independent republics or something much more ambitious such as a world-state (which Kant fears and rejects).

Read against the background of the two definitive articles of perpetual peace, the right or law of hospitality ascribes to the individual the status of being a right-bearing person in a world civil society or a *weltbuergerliche Gesellschaft*.[3] The discourse of hospitality moves from the language of morals to that of juridical right. No matter how limited in scope the right of hospitality may be, Kant's three articles of "Perpetual Peace," taken together, articulate principles of *legal cosmopolitanism*, according to which the individual is not only a moral being who is a member of a universal moral community but is also a person entitled to a certain status in a world civil society.[4] Referring to 'hospitality' as signifying all human rights claims which are cross-border in scope, as I have done in my lectures, may be more intelligible when viewed against the intentions of Kant's essay as a whole.

Waldron, therefore, is surely wrong when he writes: "I don't think hospitality is about states or political communities at all, whether at the level of a world republic or an individual republic. It is about relations between people and peoples, and it needs to be read in that determinedly *non*-state-centered way in order to capture the distinctive contribution it is supposed to make to Kant's practical philosophy" (emphasis in the text, 89–90). Hospitality and Kant's doctrine of cosmopolitan right are very much about *both states and civil society*; Waldron's is a false distinction. Certainly, Waldron is right in emphasizing how travel, contact and commerce expand one's moral horizons and widen the net of human interactions; Kant too, writes that to "seek access to others" (Zugang zu suchen), to present oneself to others, is a universal moral right. But none of this means that travel and commerce alone can generate a cosmopolitan spirit or that the value of individual *republics* should to be underestimated.

Kant, like David Hume and Adam Smith before him, emphasized the interdependence of civil freedom, free trade and the spread of enlightenment;[5] yet free trade alone is a necessary but insufficient condition for the spread of enlightenment and eventually cosmopolitan norms. Also needed is the development of free republics and free public spheres. "The peoples of the earth have thus entered in varying degrees into a universal community, and it has developed to the point where a violation of rights in *one part* of the world is felt *everywhere*. The idea of a cosmopolitan right is therefore not fantastic and overstrained; it is a necessary complement to the unwritten code of political and international rights, transforming it into a universal right of humanity" (emphasis in the original).[6]

Kant's transcendental condition of publicity mediates between morals and politics by assuring that no legislator can pass a law that would be incompatible with its being made public to people who fall under its jurisdiction.[7] Kant believes that such a principle of publicity is incompatible with any piece of legislation that would treat human beings as means only; the people would not accept their own instrumentalization and degradation. Injustices committed in other parts of the world would be felt by human beings everywhere, provided that as citizens of individual republics, they have access to free public spheres. Under despotic government, which does not permit a free public space of ideas, the news of injustice committed in other parts of the world may not even reach subjects of the despot, and even if it did, it is doubtful that it would fall upon ears attuned to cosmopolitan concerns. A submissive population who did not enjoy the free exchange of ideas at home would not possess that "enlarged mentality" to care for the plight of others in remote parts of the world. Cosmopolitan justice and republican politics are intimately related, for republican politics—not merely, and even not principally, the spirit of commerce—instill in one a sense for the worth of human beings and the justice due to all of them. The transcendental principle of publicity applies at the cosmopolitan level no less than at the level of bounded communities.

The interdependence of republican principles of government with those of trade, contact, and travel is evident for Kant at each step of the articulation of cosmopolitan right. Nevertheless, it has been widely noted that Kant's discussion of the right of hospitality does not read like a paean to free trade, but much more like a jeremiad against Western imperialism.[8] This critique of western imperialist practices—pace Waldron—is very much a critique of "the behavior of states or national conquerors" as well as of trading companies, which, at that point in time, either represented states or acted under charters sanctioned by states under various kinds of legal construction.[9] Nevertheless, Waldron and I agree that, despite all the injustices and cruelties that western imperialism brought to other parts of the world, Kant defended the universal moral right of people to seek contact with one another, and held out the hope that such contact in the long run would bring benefits for all and not be marked by war, hostility, and plunder alone. In calling for a federation of states under a common law, the second article of "Perpetual Peace" seeks to regulate the expanding world civil society of the eighteenth century. Unlike Waldron, I see no reason to burden Kant with a dualism of "state" versus "non-state-centric approaches," which is hardly compatible with his texts.

Most important, Waldron misconstrues the political essence of Kantian republicanism and misreads my claim that "Kant argued that cosmopolitan citizens still needed their individual republics to be citizens at all," as an affirmation of the "inherent importance of national political communities" (89). I wrote of individuals needing their *republics*, not their *nations*. I did so in view of Kant's defense of "civic patriotism." As Pauline Kleingeld explains in her article on "Kant's Cosmopolitan Patriotism," in Kant's writings we find strains of civic patriotism, nationalist patriotism and trait- or quality-based patriotism.[10] It was the strain of civic patriotism that I had in mind when referring to Kant's rejection of a world state, which, whether rightly or wrongly, he claimed would be a form of despotism. As Kleingeld notes, "Kant thus introduces the notion of patriotism in the contexts of discussing all three of the central ideas of his republicanism: freedom, equality, and independence. For Kant, patriotism and republicanism are clearly linked. . . . The republic (*res publica*, commonwealth) is regarded as serving the common good of the citizens. The citizens are regarded as free and equal individuals (and, often, as male and propertied). Civic patriotism does not imply the notion of a nation in an ethnic sense."[11]

Kleingeld carefully documents other passages in which Kant claims that common national ancestry leads and should lead to patriotism. She notes, however, that even in these contexts, Kant also defends the view that since all humans are descended from common ancestors, this justifies and necessitates cosmopolitanism. "Thus common ancestry is presented as the basis of a duty of love for one's co-nationals *and* of a duty of general love of humans."[12] In analyzing Kant's objections to a world state, I focused exclusively on the civic republican strains of his argument. In particular, as my discussion of the democratic paradox makes clear, I was concerned with the *principles of political representation and the need for closure* in democracies. I wrote of "bounded," not of "national" political communities and had nothing to say about Kant's "preference for national community" (92; a phrase which Waldron mistakenly attributes to me).

Waldron misses the import of this republican-democratic strain in my construction of the dilemma of cosmopolitan norms precisely because, for him, norms—whether legal or moral—must be viewed as emerging out of everyday practices. He writes: "The example of commerce, in other words, is appealed to as a prototype of how the mundane growth of repeated contact between different humans and different human groups can lay the foundation for the emergence of cosmopolitan norms, in a way that does not necessarily presuppose a formal juridical apparatus" (94). What kind of a claim is this? Is this a claim of history, sociology, or philosophy? Is this a thesis about the emergence of law out of custom? Of all kinds of law? Or only of some kinds of law? Surely, Waldron has a more general thesis in mind about the evolution of law than is present here. But in the context of discussing cosmopolitan norms pertaining to the rights of individuals in a world civil society, this claim strikes me as being singularly unconvincing. As Will Kymlicka notes in his contribution to this volume, all empirical studies of genocide and ethnic cleansing point to the paradox that it is often neighbors rather than distant strangers who massacre one another.[13] "Mundane and repeated contact" among different human groups is absolutely no guarantee of the spread of a cosmopolitan point of view that considers all human beings as individuals equally entitled to certain rights.

Waldron cites Hannah Arendt's remarks about the growth of international human rights law as a mistaken assessment of the significance of this movement. Certainly, one cannot avoid noting the bitterness with which Arendt registered the futility of "attempts to arrive at a new bill of human rights ... sponsored by marginal figures." She probably had in mind Ralph Lemkin, a tragic historical figure who fought against his own marginality and whose heroic efforts eventually led to the passing of the Genocide Convention.[14] Yet Waldron reads Arendt's comments as propounding a mistaken view about the coming into effect of universal human rights legislation and maybe of all legislation in general and comments "that its coming-into-being would involve not the thunderous imposition of positive law from on high but *the accretion and gradual crystallization of materials* such as these" (96, my emphasis).

Several recent volumes documenting the emergence of cosmopolitan norms such as crimes against humanity and the genocide convention make me question Waldron's ideal-typical presentation of the genesis of cosmopolitan law. In *A Problem from Hell: America and the Age of Genocide*, Samantha Power documents how, in fact, far from "the accretion and crystallization of materials such as these," the adoption of the Genocide Convention was an extremely contentious affair that did require the "thunderous imposition of positive law" in many cases but that failed in others. Southern lawmakers in the U.S. Senate, concerned that the Genocide Convention would apply retroactively to past slavery in the United States, thus declaring it a "crime against humanity," filibustered the discussion, with the consequence that the U.S. Senate did not ratify the Convention on the Prevention and Punishment of the Crime of Genocide until 19th of February 1986, although the Convention had been signed under President Truman (in 1948). In 1987, Congress enacted it into law in the form of "The Genocide Convention Implementation Act of 1987."[15] Although one can assume that political, moral, and cultural attitudes toward crimes against humanity and genocide had started changing much before this point,[16] as a theory of the emergence of legislation, Waldron's brief remarks on "accretion and crystallization" do not convince. I also should add that the matter of the genesis or provenance of norms in general, whether legal or sociological, was not my concern in the Tanner Lectures. I was discussing cosmopolitan norms as they became incorporated into international law through the categories of crimes against humanity, war crimes, and the genocide convention, as well as documents such as the 1951 Geneva Convention on the Status of Refugees and its Protocol added in 1967.[17]

As a general strategy, Waldron wants to blur the sharp separations between municipal law and cosmopolitan norms,[18] between the philosophical validity of the latter and their sociological effectiveness, between "formal democratic legitimacy" and "the more demotic legitimacy of ordinary iteration." Furthermore, he argues that

"Norms emerge in the world in the circumstances of dense interaction that occur *all over the place*" (98, emphasis in the text). Waldron conflates the two meanings of validity as normative correctness and institutional or sociological effectiveness (or facticity) and basically wants to dissolve the former into the latter.[19] This conflation of facticity and validity permeates Waldron's reply throughout and leads him not so much to *resolve* questions about the philosophical status of cosmopolitan norms as to *dissolve* them in a sea of ordinary practices. Am I mistaken in detecting in his argumentation the remnants of Wittgenstein's claim that most of our philosophical problems disappear when we realize that they are puzzles emerging out of the misuse of ordinary language and the mischaracterization of ordinary practices?[20] That is why Waldron declares that "there is no dilemma" regarding the mediation of universalist norms with the self-understanding of local communities. Would that this were so! In conclusion, I can only gesture toward the raging debate among globalist and nationalist international lawyers who appear not to have heard Waldron's solemn assurance that there is no morally consequential tension between norms emerging through national legislation and cosmopolitan norms. Many consider the spread of a human rights regime and the increasing limitations imposed on the action of sovereign states to be undemocratic and even to contradict constitutional government.[21]

Whereas Waldron wishes to make the puzzles and paradoxes of cosmopolitan norms disappear through respect for "the mundane growth of repeated contact" (94), Honig brings a level of metaphysical anxiety to cosmopolitanism that pushes it in the direction of the ever-recurring paradoxes of inclusion and exclusion, identity and difference. Honig proposes to name her vision "agonistic cosmopolitics" as opposed to my, in her view, 'tamer' version of neo-Kantian cosmopolitanism (117).

Jacques Derrida's reading of Kant on hospitality is decisive for Honig and sets the terms for her critique of my approach. In a series of illuminating essays Derrida comments on the deep ambivalence of the term 'hospitality.' He follows Emile Benveniste in pointing out that the terms *hospis* (host) and *hostes* (enemy) have common roots. One of Derrida's treatments on this question is named "Hostipitality," indicating the entanglement with one another of hostility and hospitality.[22] What interests Derrida is—for want of a better word—the 'phenomenological' interrelationship between the moment of hospitality and that of hostility. When the stranger (the guest) comes upon the shores of the other, the home of the other, there is also a moment of anxiety, generated by the undecidability of the other's (the host's) response:[23] Will I be greeted with hospitality or rejected with hostility? Will you admit me beyond the threshold or will you keep me waiting at the door and maybe even chase me away? Will you send me back to the land from which I am trying to escape? There is a moment of ominous uncertainty, of indecision, which lurks behind the 'initial' encounter with the other.

In Derrida's reading of Kant, that is why *hospitality* bestows a 'right' on the stranger—as long as his intentions are peaceful—and a 'duty' on the host to give the guest temporary sojourn. The host does not know the stranger's intentions; therefore, there needs to be mutually comprehensible indications of reciprocally peaceful intentions, but the possibility that communication will fail and that interests will clash always lurks in the background. Hospitality is interlaced with hostility. For Derrida, this interlacing continues even after the 'initial' moment of encounter; even after the other is admitted into our land, our city, our home, there is still a gap, a hiatus, between the acceptance of the other through hospitality and the rejection of him/her as one who does not 'belong' to us, who is not 'one' of us. The ambivalencies of hospitality extend beyond the initial entry of the stranger into another's land to his reception by the hosts over a period of time. This liminal condition of hospitality/hostility is, of course, exacerbated when the 'other' has no rights or very few ones and depends for the duration of his stay upon the 'beneficent contract' to be granted by the sovereign. (Cf. chapter 1.)

Guiding Derrida's reading of Kant are two interlocutors: Emmanuel Levinas and the 'phenomenology of the stranger' by Georg Simmel,[24] and the sources of the latter in Hegel's discussion of "Lordship and Bondage" in the *Phenomenology of Spirit*. Although Derrida's indebtedness to Levinas is explicit, the Simmelian and Hegelian sources of his discussion are less overt.

Like Levinas, Derrida sees hospitality not only as an anthropologically and culturally limited encounter with the stranger but also as an ethical encounter with the other, a fundamental welcoming, an unconditional receptivity toward the other. The otherness of the other is revealed in speech. Levinas parses the idea of the infinite as "attention to speech or welcome of the face, hospitality and not thematization."[25] As Suzanne Metselaar notes, "It is the welcoming of the other without the urge to annexing or incorporating him. In this respect 'transcendence means not appropriation of what is, but its respect.'"[26]

This ethical imperative of hospitality, as an act of fundamental welcoming toward the other, suffuses Derrida's reading of Kant as well and, interestingly, resituates the Kantian concept of hospitality within a discourse of the ethical that Kant himself was seeking to transcend. Yet there continues to exist and ought to exist an unbridgeable gap between the order of the ethical and that of the political, between what Levinas names 'infinite receptivity' toward and respect in the face of the other, and the more mundane and necessarily limited and circumscribed order of the politics of membership, citizenship, asylum, refuge, and so on. Derrida therefore distinguishes, as Honig observes, between the two orders that coexist in "paradoxical or aporetic relations . . . that are at once heterogeneous and inseparable."[27] In the conditional order of hospitality, in the domain of the *juridico-political*, limits are set, boundaries are established and protected with violence; asylees are turned away; refugees are denied entry and aid; citizens are denaturalized.

Even if one were to disagree with Levinas and Derrida, as I do, that hospitality ought to be considered the fundamental act of the ethical, that foundational moment of receptivity toward the other in which the ethical manifests itself,[28] I find Derrida's analysis of the two orders of hospitality, and in particular, of the suffusion of hospitality with hostility, of tremendous value. What has interested me in the decade preceding the delivery of the Tanner Lectures was precisely the conditional order of the *juridico-political* and the transformations it had undergone.[29] Honig seems to assume that because I focus on the *juridico-political* either that I am unaware of the ethical or that I obscure its force within the political. Yet I wrote at the very beginning of the first lecture that "due to the open-endedness of discourses of moral justification, there will be an inevitable and necessary tension between those moral obligations and duties resulting from our membership in bounded communities and the moral perspective that we must adopt as human beings *simpliciter*. From a universalist and cosmopolitan point of view, however, boundaries, including state borders and frontiers, require moral justification. The stipulations of discourse ethics to consider each and every human being as a moral agent with whom I can share a conversation of justification cannot be applied to the domain of political membership without the aid of further premises, nor is it necessary to do so. A discursive approach should place *significant limitations* on what can count as *morally permissible* practices of inclusion and exclusion within sovereign polities" (18–19).[30]

The orders of the unconditional and the conditioned are heterogeneous, but the ethical can and ought to inform the *juridico-political*. I seek neither *totalization* nor *transcendence*, to use Emmanuel Levinas's language, but *mediation*. I search for the mediation between the ethical and the moral, the moral and the political.[31]

As I have argued in *The Rights of Others*: "If we do not differentiate between *the moral and the ethical*, we cannot criticize the exclusionary citizenship and membership practices of specific cultural, religious and ethnic communities. If we do not differentiate between *morality and legality*, we cannot criticize the legally enacted norms of democratic majorities even if they refuse to admit refugees to their midst, turn away asylum seekers at the door and shut off their borders to immigrants. If we do not differentiate between *morality and functionality*, we cannot challenge practices of immigration, naturalization, and border control for violating our cherished moral, constitutional and even ethical beliefs."[32]

Would this strategy of mediation suffice for Honig? For Honig, my strategy of mediating the legal and the juridico-political with ethical and moral concerns is suspect because she sees the universalism I advocate not as being one of mediations but one of subsumptions: she considers every effort at mediation as one of subsumption. She writes: "This view of rights as always pointing to (or made to point) beyond themselves is deeply attractive. However, what those rights point to in Benhabib's account is not an open futurity dotted by new or emergent rights but a normative validity that launches us into a *subsumptive logic* in which new claims are assessed not in terms of the new worlds they may bring into being but rather in terms of their appositeness to molds and models already in place: incomplete, but definitive in their contours" (110). When rights are appropriated by new political actors and filled with content drawing on experiences that could not have guided those rights in their initial formulation, they open up new worlds and create new meanings. This is precisely what I had in mind when I used the concept of 'democratic iteration.' Every iteration transforms meaning, adds to it, enriches it in ever-so-subtle ways. There really is no "originary" source of meaning, or an "original" to which all subsequent forms must conform but, rather, there are historically encrusted practices of interpretation as well as action that are always open to future modifications, but always within certain constraints imposed by the weight of past practices.

Yet Honig is concerned to present my position as one of universalist subsumption[33] from the standpoint of which otherness, the unexpected, the new are marked as 'particularity,' as heterogeneity, as deviation, and as detraction. "Notwithstanding her commitments to reflexivity and revisability (written about in detail elsewhere), what changes in Benhabib's practices of democratic iteration here, notably, is the subject's relation to universalistic categories, not the categories themselves, (the universal stays universal, the particular stays particular)..." (110–111). Honig is referring here to my discussion of "l'affaire du foulard" and to the German Constitutional Court's decision concerning alien suffrage. But she has misunderstood my readings of them.

Both in the case of the scarf affair and in the case of demands for alien suffrage initiated by the city-state of Hamburg and the federal state of Schleswig-Holstein, we encounter practices of democratic iteration which resignify and transform the claim to universality of French and German citizenship. When the new immigrant Mariannes resignify the Marianne of the French Revolution by wearing the Phyrigian cap of the revolutionaries, they are reappropriating the identity of the French citizen and transforming it such as to include "new worlds," the world of migrant women from the Maghreb and Africa who have hardly been considered paradigms of the French citizen.

Honig is also inattentive to what is at stake in the German Constitutional Court's refusal to extend alien suffrage privileges to citizens of Denmark, the Netherlands, Norway, Ireland, Sweden, and Switzerland. Although she correctly notes the exclusion of Germany's by now 3.5 million guest workers of Turkish origin from this debate, she underestimates the opening created both by the admission of the German Constitutional Court itself that citizenship laws may be changed through parliamentary procedures and the following claim raised by the city-state of Hamburg: "The Federal Republic of Germany has in fact become in the last decades a country of immigration. Those who are affected by the law which is being attacked here are thus not strangers but cohabitants [Inlaender], who only lack German citizenship. This is especially the case for those foreigners of the second and third generation born in Germany." (BVerfG 83, 60, II, Nr. 4, 68). The brief filed by Hamburg differed from that filed by Schleswig-Holstein in that Hamburg did not restrict the granting of the vote to foreigners of the six states mentioned on the basis of

reciprocity alone but wanted to give the right to vote in local municipal assemblies (*Bezirksversammlungen*) to all those who had been
legal residents in Hamburg for eight years. This decision would have
included large numbers of Turkish guest workers and their children.
This case illustrates processes of democratic iteration and of the resignification of the universal, precisely because the briefs filed in Court
were not restricted to the question of who is entitled to vote but also
raised the issue of who is a German citizen and whether migrants and
their children could become German citizens at all. This process
became jurisgenerative when in fact in January 2000, the coalition of
Social-Democrats and Greens in the German Bundestag voted to
change Germany's antiquated citizenship laws from *jus sanguinis* to
jus soli.[34]

   For Honig, neither the state and its institutions nor the law and its
apparatus can be sites of democratic iterations and emancipatory
politics. There is a conflation in her analysis between the Derridean-
Hegelian dialectic of the universal and the particular with Michel
Foucault's claim that the law and the state are instances of governmentality, which repress political engagement and close off new
spaces of action and signification.[35] To elaborate: for Hegel, the universal constitutes itself as the universal by abstracting from and
negating difference; every claim to universality is thus linked to a
moment of exclusion.[36] Or every determination is a negation. One
can always engage in dialectic and show that all identity claims and
claims to universality are constituted by determinative exclusions;
difference is constitutive of identity. This strikes me as a common
claim of dialectic thinking; but whereas Hegel juxtaposed the
abstract to the concrete universal, and maintained that one could
aspire to a form of universality that did not simply dismiss the
moment of constitutive otherness, in Derrida's work and more so in
that of his followers, we lose sight of the concrete universal and are
confronted repeatedly by the dialectic of the abstract universal.[37]
Hence, universality appears as subsumption alone. But the correct
Hegelian point would be to emphasize that there is no particularity

without universality and that subsumption is ubiquitous, as all our concepts, even the simplest ones like 'tree,' do their job by abstracting from oak, fern, spruce, and maple trees and by subsuming them all under a general category. Concepts that are concrete universals do not operate by subsumption alone; they show that the particular is itself caught in the dialectic of the universal and the particular, and that the concrete universal is itself a manifestation of the contradictions *within* the particular. The concrete universal captures the dynamic process through which the particular is constituted.

Honig is not the practitioner of the concrete universal but of a negative dialectic: "Where the unconditional focuses our gaze on the remainders of new and established orders, Benhabib sees those remainders but does not assess them as such, that is, as *remainders*" (113). She is referring here to my claim that the condition of undocumented aliens, as well as of refugees and asylum seekers, remains in that murky domain between legality and illegality. Every order of citizenship, every order of membership generates classification and exclusion. But if this is a rather inevitable aspect of the democratic paradox of membership, isn't the point to mobilize all the institutional, normative, and cultural resources within the system of membership to undermine the logic of exclusions and to expose the self-contradictions of liberal universalism? Whereas I engage in an immanent critique of the tradition of moral and legal universalism, Honig practices the method of ideology critique and shows that every universality is afflicted by some particularity and difference which it, in turn, must repress. But if this is an ontological truism, how does its repeated deployment really help?

It is at this point that this Derrida-inspired negative dialectic merges with the Foucaultian critique of governmentality. Honig is not interested in the immanent critique of legal, political and administrative—in short, of institutional practices of citizenship and membership—because for her the paradox of constitutional democracy fails "to name the state, as such, as a problem for democracy" (115). One also does not see, blinded as one is, that privileging the "formal legal, state, state-like, and interstate institutions" (120) makes us lose worldliness in the Arendtian sense (a claim to which I will return later). Rising to a rhetorical crescendo, Honig writes that my cosmopolitanism is one "in which law, states, state-like and inter-state institutions are our principal addressees (in all of Benhabib's examples), our guardians, ventriloquizers, impersonators, shapers, and censors of our voice ..." (120).

If one sees the state and its institutions as agencies of repression, or in the old Althusserian language, of 'interpellation,' or in Foucault's language of 'disciplinary subjection,'[38] then of course there can be no redemptive dialectic at work in the legal sphere and the institutions of politics. I find it remarkable that Honig dismisses the *interplay* between the official public spheres of law and administration, on the one hand, and the unofficial public sphere of citizens' actions and social movements, on the other, which inform democratic iterations and jurisgenerative politics. Her endorsement of movement politics and her hostility toward institutions are influenced by Michel Foucault's own rather one-sided analysis of modern power as a form of governmentality that reduces citizens to objects of state administration, control, domestication, and normalization. Surely, this response is not the site in which to engage in a full discussion of the merits of the Foucaultian concepts of power and the state versus a reformulated theory of public sphere. Others have done so at length elsewhere.[39] Proceeding from quite different paradigms, Honig and I come to different assessments of institutional power and of the potentials for transforming it.

The neglect of this institutional dimension leads Honig to a rather narrow vision of agonistic cosmopolitics: the enactment of underground railroads; the designation of some spaces as cities of refuge; standing up for the 'droits de cité' as a demand to extend hospitality to refugees and other nonimmigrants who have crossed borders; these are presented as genuine sites of the political, not preempted by the state (117–118). Why should all these practices, which I also endorse, be offered *in lieu of* rather than *alongside* with, the following: fighting in various juridical spaces such as the European Court of Human

Rights for the protection of the human and civil rights of undocumented aliens? Fighting within individual polities for narrowing the
gap between the rights of citizens and those of long-term residents?
Fighting at the European level for the liberalization of citizenship laws
and at the international level for bringing citizenship and naturalization laws under the purview of human rights agreements? Contesting
the Dutch government's decision to extradite the tens of thousands of
'illegal aliens' currently in the Netherlands at all levels, juridical, civil,
political, and may be even through civil disobedience? Challenging
the criminalization of migratory movements and the predicament of
refugees and aliens the world over through whatever means at our
disposal? Combating the Bush Administration's abuse of the Geneva
Conventions in Guantanamo, which labeled hundreds of individuals
as 'illegal enemy combatants'? Criticizing the use of torture as a legitimate method of interrogation in Guantanamo, Abu Ghraib and elsewhere? Fighting against the erosion of our civil rights through the
provisions of the Patriot Act?

Such political struggles, which I am sure Honig would also endorse,
certainly address the state and its institutions without treating them
as "ventriloquizers, shapers and impersonators of our voice;" such
struggles mean getting serious about the political by engaging with it
at all levels of state, law and civil society. Agonistic politics of "the
holier than thou" kind ought to give up its antagonism to the state precisely for the sake of those who most need its protection. Ironically,
Derrida himself is far from splitting the political into the unholy realm
of the state and its institutions and the angelic realm of social movements. He states: "[T]he political task remains to find the best 'legislative' transaction, the best 'juridical' conditions to ensure that, in any
given situation, the ethics of hospitality is not violated [. . .] To that
end, one has to change laws, habits, phantasms, a whole 'culture.'"[40]
Changing "laws, habits, phantasms and a whole culture" is not contradictory to seeking the best legislative and juridical practices.

Throughout her essay, Honig appeals to Arendt in order to rescue
her from my state-centric construction of cosmopolitanism and on

behalf of her version of agonistic politics. Certainly, a thinker such as Hannah Arendt invites many readings and interpretations; her writings on politics are rich and textured enough to permit the identification of different strands of argumentation.[41] Yet Honig misreads Arendt on the Eichmann trial. Arendt was opposed to the misuse of the trial by the Ben Gurion government for the political purposes of educating Israel's citizenry in the horrors of the Holocaust, and, in particular, she was repulsed by the courtroom manner and legal logic of Chief Prosecutor Gideon Hausner. But she always thought that Israel had the right and the legal competence to try Eichmann; she objected to Gideon Hausner because he brought extraneous and emotional evidence into the courtroom and converted the trial into a 'show trial.' *Pace* Honig, Arendt was *very* much concerned that the Eichmann trial be as fair and as judicious as possible in all the appropriate procedural legal senses. She was against its political detractors. Arendt's views for a binational state in Palestine, hopes for which she had lost after Judah Magnes's death in 1948, were not in the foreground of her concerns while writing on the Eichmann trial.[42] Honig's own strategic deployment of Arendt as a hermeneuticist of suspicion is creative but arbitrary.

Both Bonnie Honig and Jeremy Waldron want to side-step the state and its institutions when considering cosmopolitan norms. At least as far as one subset of such norms is concerned, namely, the regulation of membership and of cross-border movements, they can only do so at their own peril. Arendt was very much aware of this danger:

Theoretically, in the sphere of international law it had always been true that sovereignty is nowhere more absolute than in matters of 'emigration, naturalization, nationality and expulsion.' . . . One is almost tempted to measure the degree of totalitarian infection by the extent to which the concerned governments use their sovereign rights of denationalization.[43]

Whereas Waldron and Honig accuse me of state-centrism, Kymlicka is closer to my concerns when he notes an ambivalence in my text between the *taming* of the liberal nation-state and its *transcendence*.

Agreeing with me that contemporary developments in Europe and elsewhere "challenge our most basic ideas of the nature of political community and of membership within it" (128), Kymlicka presents an alternative empirical as well as normative account of these trends. Whereas I see in the spread of the institutions of the European Union and the disaggregation of citizenship rights an advance toward legal and political cosmopolitanism, Kymlicka interprets these development as the "taming" rather than as the "transcending" of liberal nationhood (131).

In Kymlicka's view, the model of liberal nationhood, which conjoins a liberal-democratic understanding of citizenship with a national conception of membership, has been a remarkable success in ensuring democracy, economic prosperity, peace, and security for ever-increasing numbers of people in the last two centuries. By moving toward a more multicultural view of citizenship and a more multination view of belonging, along with subjecting itself to multilateral treaties and organizations in the areas of peace and security, the liberal nation-state has mitigated some of its worst aspects: discrimination against immigrants; suppression and dispossession of native and indigenous peoples on its territory and belligerence toward its neighbors (130). This is named "taming liberal nationhood." One of Kymlicka's most provocative claims is that the European Union since the mid-1950s has been in fact spreading liberal nationhood throughout Europe, but in particular, throughout its southern (Greece, Spain, Portugal, and Italy) and central-European regions (Hungary, Slovakia, Slovenia, the Czech Republic, and Poland).

There is much to commend in Kymlicka's views, but if Honig has too much metaphysical anxiety about the liberal democratic nation-state, Kymlicka has too little. In particular, there are a series of contradictions, historical tensions and even institutional disjunctions in the composite called the 'liberal-democratic nation state' that houses Kymlicka's ideal of liberal nationhood. Kymlicka begins by conflating nationality and peoplehood. He writes: "The nation-state has been seen as the privileged locus for political participation, self-government, and solidarity.

If democracy is the rule 'of the people,' then it is the nation that defines 'the people' who are to rule themselves. We exercise self-determination through electing national legislatures, and our citizenship rights are protected by national constitutions" (129, emphasis mine). We could read the italicized sentence in a voluntaristic or a substantialistic sense: read voluntaristically,[44] the nation would have to refer to all those *franchised* members of the political community who decide on the scope, extent, and boundaries of the people. But there is a circularity here: the franchised citizens decide on who the "people" are who are entitled to rule themselves, but the definition of being a franchised citizen is being part of the people. In my first lecture, I named this the paradox of democratic legitimacy, namely, that the franchised citizens would be the ones deciding upon their self-constitution by delineating between aliens and citizens. However, on this reading, it is gratuitous to refer to the nation as distinct from the people. They are one and the same.

Read substantialistically, however, the nation is distinct from the people and does not refer primarily to those who enjoy the democratic franchise but rather to a collectivity whose members share language, history, common ancestry, memories and attachment to a particular piece of land. To use the rather evocative language of the German Constitutional Court, the nation here refers to a "*Schicksalsgemeinschaft*," a community of fate. "The vision of the people of the state [*Staatsvolkes*], which underlies this right of belonging to the state, is the political community of fate [*die politische Schicksalsgemeinschaft*], to which individual citizens are bound. Their solidarity with and their embeddedness in [*Verstrickung*] the fate of their home country, which they cannot escape [*sich entrinnen koennen*], are also the justification for restricting the vote to citizens of the state."[45] According to this view, analytically, even if not historically, the political community of fate, or the nation, precedes the democratic people and constitutes the substrate of the democratic state. Which version of the nation—voluntaristic or substantialistic—does Kymlicka have in mind?

His concept of "liberal nationhood" defends a "thin" concept of nationalism; but if he also wants to hold that it is "the nation that defines 'the people' who are to rule themselves," Kymlicka cannot ignore the likelihood that the rather more "thick" understanding of the nation as a "political community of fate" would discriminate against others who are viewed as not belonging to it. By 'nation,' Kymlicka either simply means *all* citizens of a specific nation-state, or he means that collectivity of fate among citizens through whose cultural and ethnic heritage the state is defined. Parsing out these concepts is important because Kymlicka writes of liberal nationhood as if liberalism belonged to the specificity of being a nation, whereas, in my view, nations may be liberal at certain points in their history and illiberal, bigoted, and intolerant at others. Liberalism and nationalism are historically related currents of the modern world but by no means coterminous with one another.[46]

Even more important, identifying the democratic people with the nation occludes the rights of those who may not belong to the dominant nation and who may have shared in its "community of fate" only in attenuated fashion. *The principle of democracy*, namely that the people are not only the *object* but also the *authors* of the law to which they are subject, this principle of public autonomy, is distinct from national belonging, though in the vast majority of modern states that are also nation-states, there is a significant overlap between the nation and the people. The substantialistic understanding of the nation has served historically to disenfranchise some and to exclude them from the orbit of full democratic citizenship. Analytically, therefore, it is crucial to distinguish among these terms with full consciousness of the fact that behind these analytical distinctions lie historical struggles of inclusion and exclusion. Citizenship and naturalization are sites where the disjunctions between nationhood and democratic peoplehood become most apparent.

Terms such as 'liberal nationhood,' the 'nation-state,' and 'liberal democracy' are concrete universals in the Hegelian sense in that they refer to concrete totalities which contain within themselves contradictory normative principles: not only has there been conflicts between liberalism and democracy, between the protection of individual rights and the extension of the collective franchise, but there have been and will continue to be conflicts between liberalism and nationalism, and even between the state, as an organ of the rule of law, and the nation, as a political community of fate that may instrumentalize the state for the aspirations of one nation to dominate over other nationalities and peoples also living within the territories of the state. Proceeding from such conflictual totalities I ask: which polities best permit the exercise of the democratic principle? Which polities most cultivate the republican virtues of public participation and deliberation? Certainly, justice, as John Rawls has reminded us,[47] is the chief virtue of our political institutions, but justice cannot be attained without democratic citizens who are attuned to the republican virtues of participation and deliberation.

Where Kymlicka and I converge, and where we depart from Honig and Waldron, is in our emphasis on the necessity for representative *public institutions* at the statal, interstatal, and transstatal levels to be operative in order to achieve cosmopolitan norms as well as values. Political actors need bounded communities—whether they be cities, regions, states or transnational institutions—within which they can establish mechanisms of representation, accountability, participation and deliberation. For the majority of human beings, these institutions are not only sites, in the sense of *spaces* (des lieux), but also *places*, that is sites of attachment and sites of memory (lieux de mémoires). Furthermore, institutions themselves are bearers of historical memory. Kymlicka is right when he writes that democratic iterations and jurisgenerative politics require the sites provided by liberal democracies to flourish.

Borrowing a phrase from Jürgen Habermas, in the second lecture I wrote of "the Janus face of the modern nation-state," namely, that all modern nation-states that enshrine universalistic principles into their constitutions are also based on the cultural, historical, and legal memories, traditions, and institutions of a particular people and peoples. Democratic iterations and jurisgenerative politics always occur against the background of such horizons of identity and institutions. The democratic iterations of cosmopolitan norms are suffused with historically specific content, and it is this dialectic of universalistic form and particular content which we find reenacted in so many of the contemporary debates concerning immigration and citizenship. Certainly, few other political philosophers have been as attentive to the exclusionary dynamics of the cultural policies of the liberal state and so hopeful about its promises for inclusion via democratic iterations as Will Kymlicka has. Nonetheless, various developments within the EU and the disaggregation of citizenship rights have created dynamics that may not be neatly contained within the model of liberal nationhood.

Whereas Kymlicka sees the European Union as a vehicle for spreading liberal nationhood (131), I think that the institutional structures that constitute the EU point to a far more ambitious devolution of sovereignty. European Union law takes precedence over domestic law, even if with continuing conflict of interpretations, in all but one domain: immigration, naturalization, and admission of refugees and asylum seekers. There is an open method of coordination in these areas but no EU-wide legislation. Otherwise, the European Union has progressed far beyond an intergovernmental model of organization toward a consociation of states that is poised between a federal model and a looser association whose precise form is yet to be determined. Clearly, the recent defeat of the EU Constitution in the hands of French and Dutch voters in the summer of 2005 is a plain sign of discontent as well as disorientation about this newly emerging structure. In fact, on a first reading these developments support Kymlicka's point about the depth and tenacity of liberal nationhood and disappoint more cosmopolitan federalist hopes which I shared with many others. However, the institutional dynamic within the EU is so powerful that, even with the negative votes on the Constitution, it is unlikely that there will be a devolution toward more national sovereignty; most likely, the momentum toward a multinational federalist EU is stalled but not stopped. If conservative parties come to power in the next few years in Germany and France, as is very likely, those who want to "deepen" the EU institutions will prevail over those who would like to "widen" them. Be that as it may, I would still contend that even in the absence of a constitution, the various Treaties of the European Union have established a composite structure that goes far beyond a trade pact or an intergovernmental organization toward a new form of pooling and transcending national sovereignty.[48]

But is this new structure the site of cosmopolitan consciousness? Honig, as well as Kymlicka, note the ethnocentric, racist, and exclusivist trends within the new European Union. I also have documented in various writings how the establishment of the European Union has been accompanied by a tightening of immigration controls and increasingly more restrictive interpretations of the rights of refugees and asylum seekers.[49] Given the increasingly hostile security environment since the Iraq War and the reality of fundamentalist Islamic terrorism in Europe, pan-Europeanism may not result in heightened cosmopolitan consciousness but in a new form of chauvinism, heavily interlaced with racist attitudes toward the Muslim world.[50]

A central contention of my Tanner Lectures was that the disaggregation of citizenship, which unbundled entitlement to civil, social, and some political rights from national belonging, was one of the clearest indicators of the evolution of cosmopolitan norms. This is most obviously the case for all citizens of member nations of the European Union who can settle in other member countries (subject to certain market restrictions), who can assume residency and vote, as well as stand for candidacy, in local and European Union–wide elections. For the EU's third-country nationals, as well, not only does the entitlement to social rights such as unemployment, health care and retirement benefits depend on long-term residency rather than citizenship status, but so does the entitlement to participate in local and regional elections in Sweden, Denmark, the Netherlands, Ireland, Finland, and, to a lesser extent, in Spain, Portugal, and in the United Kingdom.[51]

Kymlicka queries whether this unbundling of rights is an *alternative to* or *step toward* national citizenship; he endorses it on the following proviso: "Temporary unbundling is politically progressive if and when it serves as a step towards rebundling in the form of full and equal citizenship within the framework of liberal nationhood" (139). He wishes to view local voting rights as a "proto-citizenship right," "enabling immigrants to develop bonds of trust and attachment towards national institutions, and hence as a step towards full national citizenship" (139).

Kymlicka is surely correct that the unbundling of rights should in no way be considered an alternative to the acquisition of full citizenship. To be sure, I also endorse the liberalization of naturalization laws throughout the member countries of the EU. However, I do not share his teleological focus on national citizenship as the end goal toward which the disaggregation of rights ought to evolve. Nonnational modes of belonging, such as long-term residency or denizenship, binationality, and transnationality are among some of the alternatives currently evolving, not only in Europe, but throughout the world as well. Along with these changes, the site of political activity is decentered: proto-citizenship rights can be exercised at local and regional as well as supra- and transnational levels. The nation-state is not the sole site of our democratic attachments. Kymlicka once more conflates the democratic principle of public autonomy with the principle of national belonging, whereas I see different modalities of non-national citizenship arising *along with* rather than *in place of* national citizenship.

Why? Why not follow the more traditional perspective defended by Kymlicka and see the unbundling of rights as a step toward full national citizenship? Within the European context there is first and foremost a matter of *fairness* toward long-term resident third-country nationals of non-EU member countries. Whereas nationals of EU member countries can acquire EU citizenship, third-country nationals cannot do so unless and until they become naturalized in one of the member countries. I would like to see third-country nationals acquire EU citizenship without having to first accept national membership. They would still have to fulfill certain criteria such as residency within EU borders in one or more countries over a period of time; show competence in *one* of the officially recognized languages of the European Union (for many individuals it may be easier to prove competency in English than in German or Danish); prove knowledge of European Union institutions along with knowledge of the history and institutions of the country in which they wish to officially reside. Naturalized European Union citizens ought to be entitled to the same rights as all other EU citizens.

To give a few illustrations of how this may work: a Moroccan child, born and raised in Barcelona, today can acquire EU citizenship only by first becoming a Spanish citizen. But why should national citizenship be a requirement for participating in European-level institutions rather than the socialization and integration already received in a strongly independent region of Spain, which has its own national language? Likewise, why can a Turkish child born in Koln, Germany, have to be abdicate her Turkish citizenship at age twenty-four, if she can apply for European Union citizenship via proving competency in English as well as a working knowledge of German? The question as to whether or not the European Union ought to permit dual nationality with Morocco or Turkey can be answered at the next level. Thus, I disagree with Kymlicka when he assumes "that being a citizen of Berlin and Europe is not an acceptable alternative to being a citizen of Germany" (140). Why not indeed?[52] One can be an extremely active citizen of the city of Berlin, participate in local elections, organize at the cultural and political levels and take part in European Union elections, provided that there are also genuinely pan-European parties and not merely platforms of candidates presented by national parties for election to the European Parliament. The disaggregation of citizenship rights points toward the formation of trans- and supranational institutions as well.

What is the link between formal citizenship and nationhood? To what extent is it really possible to disassociate, as I want to do, democratic citizenship from nationality? How are the *ethnos* and the *demos* related? Kymlicka believes that the institutions of liberal nationhood have integrated ethnos and demos in a beneficial and progressive way for most human beings over a period of two hundred years. Historically, of course, the formation of the nation has also been accompanied by repressions, exclusions, massacres, and battles. Kymlicka is aware of this and asks why continental European countries such as France and Germany are so reluctant to accept more multicultural conceptions of liberal nationhood. In his view, "at best, these countries are slouching towards this model, at worst they are moving away from it"(141). Another alternative would be the renegotiation of the boundaries between ethnos and demos such that the core nation reconstitutes itself in more universalistic terms, expands immigrants' civil and political rights, liberalizes asylum and refugee policies, provides amnesty for undocumented aliens, creates socioeconomic equality and free access to public schooling for immigrant communities, while recognizing that the immigrant is not simply the 'other,' but one who has also made an intrinsic contribution to the formation of the nation. Despite their continuing ideologies of nationhood, there is no nation in Europe which has not been formed through inter- and intra-European migration. Some sense of the fluidity about the formation of the nation would be essential to this process.[53]

Multiculturalism in contemporary Europe concerns not only ethnicity but also, and very prominently, class. Europe's 'others' are not primarily North or South Americans, Australians, and Canadians, but citizens of third-world countries from the Middle East, from all over Africa but especially its northern region, from Asia and, increasingly, from the countries of the former Yugoslavia. The majority of these individuals constitute Europe's *lumpen proletariat*, despite the occasional presence of professionals and business owners among them. As European social democracy has shrunk in the last decades under the impact of global economic competition, the costs of German unification and the dislocations caused by the common Euro-market, these groups have become subject not only to continuous discrimination but also to socioeconomic cutbacks and increasing unemployment. In the current context, it is desirable to find a language of universalistic solidarity which also would be a language of integration through socioeconomic equality rather than that of assimilation through denial of difference. Redistribution and recognition struggles need to go hand in hand. This process may move the liberal nation toward the more democratic kind of cosmopolitanism that I have proposed in these lectures.

I began these lectures with the observation that the term cosmopolitanism has become a key word of our times. Whether cosmopolitanism is used to designate the hybridity, fluidity, intermingling, and interdependence of peoples, cultures, and practices, or a process of taming the nation-state such as to control the assertion of unbridled sovereignty, or even a politics of hospitality that challenges existing liberal democracies in order to examine their deepest self-understandings, this term and its derivates such as 'cosmopolitics' grapple with the unique challenges of our times. These are in the first place the incongruity between the level of commercial, technological and functional interdependence of the world community on the one hand and the continuing role of sovereign statehood in defining the juridical status of individual human beings on the other. Universal legal personality remains a chimera in our days, as much as it was in Kant's, with the added problem that the predatory and destructive capacities of states and non-state agents have vastly increased in the centuries since 1795 when Kant penned "Perpetual Peace." Despite recent enthusiasm for the development of 'global law without the state,'[54] the state remains the distributor and guarantor of human rights. The individual who is stateless, in our times as much as in Arendt's, becomes a nonperson, a body that can be moved around by armies and police, customs officers and refugee agencies. Wouldn't perhaps a truly cosmopolitan politics require that every human child receive a passport as a world citizen in addition to his/her local identification papers? Doesn't the category of 'crimes against humanity' suggest that the human person ought to be given universal legal personhood?

Second, whether we seek to tame the nation-state or to transcend it, there are certain developments through which the state is devolving its own powers and thus posing great dangers to its citizens. This devolution of the state's regulatory capacities is taking place, in large measure, as a consequence of the exigencies of global capitalism. The model of liberal sovereignty, based on the unity of jurisdiction administered over a defined territory, assuring citizen's equality through the administration of the rule of law, more and more appears as if it were the memory of a quaint past. As Bill Scheuerman notes in *Liberal Democracy and the Social Acceleration of Time:*

Contemporary capitalism is different in many ways from its historical predecessors: economies driven by huge transnational corporations that make effective use of high-speed communication, information, and transportation technologies represent a relatively novel development. The relationship of capitalism to the rule of law is thereby transformed as well.... As high-speed social action 'compresses' distance, the separation between domestic and foreign affairs erodes, and the traditional vision of the executive as best suited to the dictates of rapid-fire foreign policy making undermines basic standards of legality in the domestic sphere as well.[55]

The transformation of the rule of law gives rise to 'fast-track legislation,' pushed by national legislators without adequate debate and deliberation; the power of deliberative bodies is eclipsed and that of the executive increases. Administrative discretion comes to replace general legislation.

Ironically, sovereign states are players with considerable power in this process: they themselves often nurture and guide the very transformations which curtail or limit their own powers. Whether it be through the emergence of new global forms of law without a state in the accelerated and fluid global market place or through the pressure to adopt state bureaucracies to the new capitalism, an epochal change is under way in which aspects of state sovereignty are being dismantled chip by chip. State jurisdiction and territoriality are uncoupled, as new agents of jurisdiction in the form of multinational corporations emerge. In some cases, the state disburses its own jurisdiction to private agencies in order to escape the territorial control of popular legislators. The social contract is increasingly frayed.

The fraying of the social contract and the dismantling of sovereignty suggest that the transcendence of the nation-state is occurring hardly in the direction of cosmopolitanism but more in the direction of the privatization and corporatization of sovereignty. These trends endanger democracy and popular sovereignty by converting public power into private commercial or administrative competence. Democracies' abilities to regulate the actions that are taken in their name are increasingly weakened. This is the truth behind contemporary theories of empire: the flight of power from the control of popular jurisdiction.

With the concept of 'democratic iterations,' I wanted to signal forms of popular empowerment and political struggle through which the people themselves would appropriate the universalist promise of cosmopolitan norms in order to bind forms of political and economic power that seek to escape democratic control, accountability and transparency. The interlocking of democratic iteration struggles within a global civil society and the creation of solidarities beyond borders, including a universal right of hospitality that recognizes the other as a potential cocitizen, anticipate another cosmopolitanism—a cosmopolitanism to come.

Notes

1. Katrin Flikschuh, *Kant and Modern Political Philosophy* (Cambridge: Cambridge University Press, 2000), p. 184. For further discussion of Kant' cosmopolitan right, see Seyla Benhabib, *The Rights of Others: Aliens, Residents and Citizens* (Cambridge: Cambridge University Press, 2004), pp. 25–35.

2. I have used the following Kant editions: Immanuel Kant, "Zum Ewigen Frieden: Ein philosophischer Entwurf" [1795], *in Immanuel Kants Werke (Shriften von 1790–1796)*, ed. A. Buchenau, E. Cassirer and B. Kellermann (Berlin: Verlag Bruno Cassirer, 1923), pp. 425–474. Referred to in the text as "Kant [1795] 1923"; Immanuel Kant, "Perpetual Peace: A Philosophical Sketch" [1795], trans. H. B. Nisbet, in *Kant: Political Writings*, ed. Hans Reiss, 2nd and enl. ed. (Cambridge: Cambridge University Press, 1994), pp. 93–131. Referred to in the text as "Kant [1795] 1994." Kant [1795] 1923, pp. 434–446; [1795]1994, pp. 99–108.

3. Ingeborg Maus notes convincingly that Kant's conception of cosmopolitan right (Weltbuergerrecht) is neither state-centric nor individualistically oriented but is based upon the complex interaction of both: "Kant's cosmopolitan right, therefore, does not designate a supranational order; rather, it partially anticipates modern international personal law (Internationales Privatrecht), which is based on the simultaneity of national systems of law and international transactions among private individuals. There can be a collision among these realms and when the question arises, which legal norm of which concerned state must be recognized as valid in a concrete instance, this can only be answered by presupposing extraterritorial juridical validity." Ingeborg Maus, "Vom Nationalstaat zum Globalstaat oder: der Niedergang der Demokratie," ("From the Nation-State to the Global-State or the Decline of Democracy"), in *Weltstaat oder Staatenwelt: Fuer und Wider die Idee einer Wletrepublik*, edited by Matthias Lutz-Bachmann and James Bohman (Franfurt: Suhrkamp, 2002), pp.226–259; here p. 233. I thank Thomas A. McCarthy for conversations around this point.

4. In his comprehensive treatment of the rights of strangers, which extends from Vitoria and the Second Scholastic to Kant and contemporary issues, Georg Cavallar takes issue with readings of Kant's right of hospitality as "anticipating a global and democratic civil society" (Georg Cavallar, *The Rights of Strangers: Theories of International Hospitality, the Global Community and Political Justice since Vitoria* [(Aldershot: Ashgate, 2002], pp. 361). He disagrees with the thesis that the cosmopolitan public sphere as 'negative substitute' can take over the provisional controls of international relations and move toward a post-Westphalian order. Cavallar maintains that since "rights violations which are not attributable to state actors are difficult to prevent and enforce," saddling Kant with wanting to do away with the coercive power of republics, is not

helpful (pp. 362–363). Yet while not wanting to dismiss "globalist inter-pretations out of hand," Cavallar admits that the import of the third definitive article of perpetual peace is to establish a civil constitution, "complementing (again: not replacing) domestic and international right" (p. 363). I believe that Cavallar exaggerates the extent to which globalists such as James Bohman and David Held want to do away with the state. Post-Westphalian models of sovereignty do not presuppose the withering away of the state (24ff.). As I also explicate in my response to Kymlicka, I certainly am not advocating the 'transcendence' of the state but rather its 'transformation.' This is the intent of my call for 'cosmopolitan federal-ism.' See Benhabib, *The Rights of Others*, pp. 215–221.

Cavallar's excellent study, however, made me realize the extent to which Franciso de Vitoria's doctrine of hospitality anticipated much of Kant and was in fact more daring than Kant's views to the extent to which Vitoria included the *jus solis*, or freedom of residence, naturalization and citizenship, and the negation of a right of expulsion without a just cause, under the right of hospitality. At this stage, I have not been able to ascer-tain whether or not Kant was familiar with Vitoria. Cavallar leaves this also open. See Cavallar, *The Rights of Strangers*, pp. 107–112.

5. Cf. "For *the spirit of commerce* sooner or later takes hold of every peo-ple, and it cannot exits side by side with war. And of all the powers (or means) at the disposal of the power of the state, *financial power* can be relied on most" ("Perpetual Peace," in *Kant: Political Writings*, ed. H. Reiss, p. 114). In these passages, Kant is speculating about how the mechanisms of "nature" (meaning here teleological developments in society and history as well) may help the cause of perpetual peace. His remarks on European imperialism in the preceding sections of the essay make clear, however, that even the spirit of commerce cannot overcome human bellicosity, see "Perpetual Peace," pp. 106–108 and 111.

6. Kant, "Perpetual Peace," in *Kant: Political Writings*, ed. by Hans Reiss, pp. 107–108.

7. See the "transcendental formula of public right": "All actions affect-ing the rights of other human beings are wrong if their maxim is not com-patible with their being made public. . . . [T]his principle should be regarded not only as *ethical* (i.e. pertaining to the theory of virtue) but also as *juridical* (i.e. affecting the rights of man)," in "Perpetual Peace," in *Kant: Political Writings*, p. 126.

8. Cf. Sankar Muthu, *Enlightenment against Empire* (Princeton, N.J.: Princeton University Press, 2003); Pauline Kleingeld, "Kant's Cosmopolitan Law: World Citizenship for a Global Order," *Kantian Review* 2 (1998), pp. 72–90; for a review of the recent literature on this issue, see Mirko Wischke, "Die Politik der Menschenrechte im Zeitalter der Globalisierung: Zur aktuellen Diskussion in der Politischen Philosophie und Rechtsphilosophie," *Philosophische Rundschau* 49, pp. 224–244.

9. For a masterful account of the dialectic of imperialism and legal constructions of international law, see Martti Koskenniemi, *The Gentle Civilizer of Nations: The Rise and Fall of International Law 1870–1960* (Cambridge: Cambridge University Press, 2001), pp. 143–179 in particular.

10. Pauline Kleingeld, "Kant's Cosmopolitan Patriotism," *Kant-Studien* 94 (2003), pp. 299–316; here pp. 303–305.

11. Ibid., p. 304

12. Ibid., p. 304. Her references are to Kant's *Gesammelte Schriften*, vol. XXVII. 2, 1, 673.

13. Kymlicka writes: ". . . national identities are often defined precisely by antagonism to neighboring nations, creating the potential for inter-state rivalries and hostilities." He refers to Nenad Misevic, "Close Strangers: Nationalism, Proximity and Cosmopolitanism, *Studies in European Thought* 51 (1999): 109–125.

14. See Samantha Power, *A Problem from Hell: America and the Age of Genocide* (New York: Basic Books, 2003), pp. 31–60.

15. The legislation became known as "the Proxmire Act" (Public Law 100–606), after Senator Proxmire, who had tirelessly fought for its ratification. President Reagan signed it into law on November 4th 1988 (18 U.S.C. 1091). Available at: http://thomas.loc.gov/cgi-bin/query/D?c108:1:./temp/~c108wWBOye. Power writes: ". . . American opposition was rooted in a traditional hostility toward any infringement on U.S. sovereignty, which was only amplified by the red scare of the 1950s. If the United States ratified the pact, senators worried that they would thus authorize outsiders to poke around in the internal affairs of the United States or embroil the country in an 'entangling alliance.' Power, *A Problem from Hell: America and the Age of Genocide*, p. 69.

16. There is a considerable literature about the impact of the news of the Holocaust in particular upon the socialization and formation of post-World War II German youth, beginning with Alexander Mitscherlich's classic,

Society without the Father: A Contribution to Social Psychology, trans. Eric Mosbacher (New York: Schocken Books [1963] 1970); for the American reception, see Jeffrey S. Alexander, "On the Social Construction of Moral Universals: The 'Holocaust' from War Crime to Trauma Drama," pp. 27–84 in Jeffrey C. Alexander, *The Meanings of Social Life: A Cultural Sociology* (New York: Oxford, 2004).

17. I have discussed the legal evolution of these norms in greater detail in Benhabib, *The Rights of Others*, pp. 8–10 and 68–70.

18. My views on this matter follow Gerald Neuman, who notes that some state constitutions are monistic and accept valid international law as national law, while others are dualistic and distinguish between domestic law and international law and do not incorporate them into their constitutions. See G. Neumann, "Human Rights and Constitutional Rights: Harmony and Dissonance." *Stanford Law Review* 55 (2003): 1863–1901.

19. See Jürgen Habermas, *Between Facts and Norms*, trans. W. Regh (Cambridge, Mass.: MIT Press, 1996) for an elucidation of the distinction between "facticity" and "validity."

20. Ludwig Wittgenstein, *Philosophical Investigations*, the German text, with a revised English translation; trans. G. E. M. Anscombe (Malden, Mass.: Blackwell, 2001).

21. For a most recent exchange see Jed Rubenfeld, "The Two World Orders" and Anne-Marie Slaughter, "Leading Through Law," *The Wilson Quarterly*, Special Section on "What Good is International Law?" (Autumn 2003), pp. 22–36 and 42–43, respectively. For a learned diatribe against the spread of international law and cosmopolitan norms, which sees in the European Union the fulfillment of fantasies of empire and pleads for the United States to distance itself from postnationalist servility, see Jeremy A. Rabkin, *Law Without Nations: Why Constitutional Government Requires Sovereign States* (Princeton, N.J.: Princeton University Press, 2005).

22. See Jacques Derrida, *Of Hospitality: Anne Dufourmantelle Invites Jacques Derrida to Respond*, trans. Rachel Bowlby (Stanford: Stanford University Press, 2000); *Adieu to Emmanuel Levinas* (Stanford: Stanford University Press, 1999); *On Cosmopolitanism and Forgiveness*, trans. Mark Dooley and Michael Hughes (London and New York: Routledge, 2001); "The Principle of Hospitality," An Interview with Dominique

Dhombres for *Le Monde* (December 2, 1997), trans. Ashley Thompson in *Parallax* 11 (Special Issue on Seeking Asylum, January-March 2005), Guest Editor Obrad Savic, pp. 6–10; and "Hostipitality": in *Acts of Religion*, edited by Gil Anidjar (New York: Routledge, 2002), pp. 356–420.

23. The positions of the host and the guest are interchangeable in the philosophical account; each guest can be a host and vice versa, but of course, in the sociological register, these positions are determined by race, class, gender, ethnic and geographical distinctions. But at the phenomenological level of everyday encounter among two subjects, the reversibility of positions is as crucial for Derrida as it was for Hegel's account of "Lordship and Bondage" in *The Phenomenology of Spirit*. See G. W. F. Hegel, *Phaenomenologie des Geistes* [1807], in *Hegels Werke* (Felix Meiner Verlag: 1956); trans. A. V. Miller, and Analysis of the Text and Foreword by J. N. Findlay; A. V. Miller, *Phenomenology of Spirit* (Clarendon Press: Oxford, 1977), pp. 111–119.

24. Cf. Georg Simmel, "The Stranger" [1908], in *The Sociology of Georg Simmel*, trans. Kurt H. Wolff (Glencoe, Ill: Free Press, 1950) pp. 402–408.

25. Emmanuel Levinas, *Totality and Infinity, an Essay on Exteriority*, trans. Alphonso Lingis (Pittsburgh, Pa.: Duquesne University Press, 1969)

26. Suzanne Metselaar, "When Neighbors Become Numbers: Levinas and the Inhospitality of Dutch Asylum Policy," in *Parallax* (Special Issue) 11 (January-March 2005), Guest Editor Obrad Savic, pp. 61–69, here p. 63. Metselaar is citing Levinas, *Totality and Infinity*, p. 302.

27. Jacques Derrida, *Rogues: Two Essays on Reason* (Stanford: Stanford University Press, 2005), p. 173 n. 12; cited by Honig on p. 5.

28. For my own work on the foundations of ethics and the mediation between the universal and the concrete other, see *Situating the Self: Gender, Community and Postmodernism in Contemporary Ethics* (London and New York: Routledge and Polity, 1992).

29. See Benhabib, *Transformations of Citizenship: Dilemmas of the Nation-State in the Era of Globalization*. Baruch de Spinoza Lectures (Amsterdam: The University of Amsterdam, 2001) and further "Transformations of Citizenship: The Case of Contemporary Europe," *Government and Opposition: An International Journal of Comparative*

Politics 37 (Autumn 2002): 439–465. See also *The Claims of Culture: Equality and Diversity in the Global Era* (Princeton, N.J.: Princeton University Press, 2002), chap. 6; for earlier statements, see "Dismantling the Leviathan: Citizen and State in a Global World," *The Responsive Community* 11, no. 3 (2001): 14–27; and "Ungrounded Fears, American Intellectuals and the Spectre of European Harmonization, A Response to Michael Walzer and Noah M. Pickus," *The Responsive Community* 11, no. 4 (2001): 85–91.

30. Honig is wrong in claiming that I was "led to cosmopolitanism by the new empirical facts of state sovereignty attenuation in the late twentieth century" (115). My interest in cosmopolitanism originates with my interest in universalistic ethics. Transformations of citizenship and sovereignty in the late twentieth century are of significance precisely because they embody some of the dilemmas of moral universalism and legal and political cosmopolitanism most vividly.

31. I do not see a clear differentiation in either Derrida's or Levinas's usages between the 'ethical' (Sittlichkeit) and 'morality' (Moralitaet). This is of great consequence for appreciating the kind of universalism I defend. See my essay "In the Shadow of Aristotle and Hegel: Communicative Ethics and Current Controversies in Practical Philosophy," in *Situating the Self*, pp. 23–68.

32. See Benhabib, *The Rights of Others*, p. 16.

33. I find it ironic that Honig would accuse me of "subsumptive universalism," after more than a decade ago I introduced the distinction between 'subsumptive' and 'interactive' universalism to characterize the distinction between Rawlsian versus dialogical models of universalism. I have not changed my position in this regard and have continued to elaborate a program of dialogic universalism. See "The Generalized and the Concrete Other," in Benhabib, *Situating the Self*, pp. 148–178.

34. See Seyla Benhabib, "Germany Opens Up," *The Nation*, June 21 1999, p. 6.

35. On Foucault and governmentality, see Michel Foucault, *Discipline and Punish*, trans. Alan Sheridan (Pantheon Books: New York, 1977); Hubert L. Dreyfus and Paul Rabinow, *Michel Foucault: Beyond Structuralism and Hermeneutics* (Chicago: University of Chicago Press, 1982); Michel Foucault, *Power/Knowledge*, ed. Colin Gordon (New York: Pantheon Books,

1980); *The Foucault Reader*, ed. Paul Rabinow (New York: Pantheon Books, 1984).

36. G. W. F. Hegel, *Hegel's Science of Logic*, trans. W. H. Johnston and L. G. Struthers (New York: Humanities Press, 1966), 4th ed., Vol. I, "First Original Law of Thought: the Law of Identity," pp. 39–43.

37. For the distinction between the abstract and concrete universal, see Hegel, *Hegel's Science of Logic*, Vol. 2, "Subjective Logic or the Doctrine of the Notion," pp. 234–257. The translators unfortunately render Hegel's term of "Begriff" as "The Notion." The more appropriate translation, which also clarifies Hegel's relation to Kant, would be simply "the concept."

38. There is a long and complicated debate in European thought since the 1970s about the status of the subject and whether a "politics beyond the subject" is necessarily emancipatory or whether such politics simply affirms the loss of agency and subjectivity experienced by individuals in late modernity. I have entered this discussion with my essay "Feminism and the Question of Postmodernism," *in Situating the Self: Gender, Community and Postmodernism*, pp. 203–242.

39. See Axel Honneth, *The Critique of Power: Reflective Stages in a Critical Social Theory*, trans. Kenneth Baynes (Cambridge, Mass.: MIT Press, 1991), Part II, 99–176; and Nancy Fraser, "Foucault on Modern Power: Empirical Insights and Normative Confusions," *Praxis International* 1 (1981), pp. 272 ff.; Jürgen Habermas, *The Philosophical Discourse of Modernity: Twelve Lectures*, trans. by Frederick Lawrence (Cambridge, Mass.: MIT Press, 1987).

40. Cited in Metselaar, "When Neighbors become Numbers," p. 68. Citing Derrida from: http://culturemachine.tees.as.uk/Cmach/Backissues/joo2/Articles/art_derr.htm.

41. See my *The Reluctant Modernism of Hannah Arendt*, 2nd edition [1996] (Lanham, Md: Rowman and Littlefield, 2002) and Bonnie Honig, "Re-Reading the Canon," in *Feminist Interpretations of Hannah Arendt*, ed. Bonnie Honig (University Park: Pennsylvania State University Press, 1995).

42. See Leora Bilsky, *Transformative Justice: Israeli Identity on Trial* (Ann Arbor: University of Michigan Press, 2004).

43. Hannah Arendt, *The Origins of Totalitarianism* (New York: Harcourt, Brace and Jovanovich, [1951] 1968), pp. 278–279.

44. I identify this voluntaristic view with Ernest Renan, "Qu'est-ce qu'une nation?" (lecture given at the Sorbonne, March 11, 1882). Available at: http://ourworld.compuserve.com/homepages/bib_lisieux/nation01.htm. English trans.: Renan, Ernest, "What is a Nation?" in *Nation and Narration*, ed. Homi K. Bhabha (New York: Routledge, 1990), pp. 8–22.

45. BVerfG 83, 37, Nr. 3, pp. 39–40.

46. For some classical treatments, see Eric Hobsbawm, *Nations and Nationalism Since 1780: Programme, Myth and Reality* (Cambridge: Cambridge University Press, 1990); Benedict Anderson, *Imagined Communities* (London: Verso, 1983); Rogers Brubaker, *Citizenship and Nationhood in France and Germany* (Cambridge, Mass.: Harvard University Press, 1992) and Rogers Brubaker, *Nationalism Reframed: Nationhood and the National Question in the New Europe* (Cambridge: Cambridge University Press, 1997).

47. John Rawls, *A Theory of Justice* (Cambridge, Mass.: Harvard University Press, 1971).

48. See the documents collected in the volume *Europa-Recht*, edited and with an Introduction by Professor Claus Dieter Classen (Deutscher Taschenbuch Verlag:Munich, 2005), 20th and revised edition, and *Die neue Verfassung fuer Europa*, edited by Rudolf Streinz, Christoph Ohler, and Christoph Herrmann (Munich: C. H.Beck, 2005). In the introduction, the authors document the oddity of the language of the EU Constitution, vacillating between that of a contract and that of a constitution, pp. 23 ff., and conclude that "member states remain 'the masters of the contracts' . . ." (25). This is admittedly an unstable construction which itself generates more juridical puzzles than it solves.

49. Seyla Benhabib, "In Search of Europe's Borders: The Politics of Migration in the European Union," *Dissent* (Fall 2002): 33–39.

50. See Etienne Balibar's compelling discussion in *We, the People of Europe? Reflections of Transnational Citizenship*, trans. James Swenson (Princeton, N.J.: Princeton University Press, 2004).

51. For a more detailed analysis of the distribution of these rights and various restrictions on them, see Benhabib, *The Rights of Others*, pp. 158–162.

52. See the debate about German multiculturalism in *Multicultural Germany: Art, Performance, and Media*, special issue of *New German Critique*, no. 92 (Spring/Summer 2004).

53. Saskia Sassen, *Guests and Aliens* (New York: The New Press, 2000); Rainer Bauboeck, *Transnational Citizenship: Membership and Rights in International Migration* (Northampton, Mass.: Edward Elgar, 1994) and Aristide R. Zollberg and Long Litt Woon, "Why Islam is like Spanish: Cultural Incorporation in Europe and the United States," *Politics and Society* 27 (March 1999): 5–38.

54. See Gunther Teubner, ed., *Global Law Without a State: Studies in Modern Law and Policy* (Brookfield, Vt.: Dartmouth Publishing Company, 1997), p. 5.

55. William. E. Scheuerman, *Liberal Democracy and the Social Acceleration of Time* (Baltimore: Johns Hopkins University Press, 2004), p. 145.

Bibliography

Agamben, Giorgio. *Homo Sacer: Sovereign Power and Bare Life* (Stanford: Stanford University Press, 1998).

Alexander, Jeffrey C. *The Meanings of Social Life: A Cultural Sociology* (New York: Oxford University Press, 2004).

Anderson, Benedict. *Imagined Communities* (London: Verso, 1983).

Arendt, Hannah. *The Origins of Totalitarianism*, new ed. with added prefaces (New York: Harcourt Brace Jovanovich, [1951, 1966] 1979).

———. *The Human Condition* (Chicago: University of Chicago Press, 1958).

———. *On Revolution* (London: Penguin Books, [1963] 1990).

———. *Hannah Arendt–Karl Jaspers Correspondence: 1926–1969*, ed. Lotte Kohler and Hans Saner, trans. Robert and Rita Kimber (New York: Harcourt Brace Jovanovich, 1992).

———. *Eichmann in Jerusalem: A Report on the Banality of Evil*, revised and enlarged ed. (New York: Penguin Books, [1963] 1994).

Balibar, Etienne. "Europe as Borderland," The Alexander von Humboldt Lecture in Human Geography, University of Nijmegen, November 10, 2004, http://www.ru.nl/socgeo/n/colloquium/Europe%20as%20 Borderland.pdf.

———. *We, the People of Europe? Reflections of Transnational Citizenship*, trans. James Swenson (Princeton, N.J.: Princeton University Press 2004).

Barber, Benjamin. *Jihad vs. McWorld* (New York: Times Books, 1995).

Bauboeck, Rainer. *Transnational Citizenship: Membership and Rights in International Migration* (Northampton, Mass.: Edward Elgar, 1994).

Benhabib, Seyla. *Situating the Self: Gender, Community and Postmodernism in Contemporary Ethics* (London and New York: Routledge and Polity, 1992).

———. *The Reluctant Modernism of Hannah Arendt*, 2nd ed. (Lanham, Md.: Rowman and Littlefield, [1996] 2002).

———. "Germany Opens Up," *The Nation*. June 21, 1999.

Benhabib, Seyla. "Dismantling the Leviathan: Citizen and State in a Global World," *The Responsive Community* 11, no. 3 (2001): 14–27.

———. "Ungrounded Fears: American Intellectuals and the Spectre of European Harmonization. A Response to Michael Walzer and Noah M. Pickus," *The Responsive Community* 11, no. 4 (2001): 85–91.

———. *Transformations of Citizenship: Dilemmas of the Nation-State in the Era of Globalization: Spinoza Lectures* (Amsterdam: Van Gorcum, 2001).

———. "In Search of Europe's Borders: The Politics of Migration in the European Union," *Dissent* (Fall 2002): 33–39.

———. "Transformations of Citizenship: The Case of Contemporary Europe," *Government and Opposition: An International Journal of Comparative Politics* 37, no. 4 (2002): 439–465.

———. *The Claims of Culture: Equality and Diversity in the Global Era* (Princeton, N.J.: Princeton University Press, 2002).

———. *The Rights of Others: Aliens, Residents and Citizens: The John Seeley Memorial Lectures* (Cambridge: Cambridge University Press, 2004).

Bilsky, Leora. *Transformative Justice: Israeli Identity on Trial* (Ann Arbor: University of Michigan Press, 2004).

Bohman, James. "The Public Spheres of the World Citizen," in *Perpetual Peace: Essays on Kant's Cosmopolitan Ideal*, ed. James Bohman and Matthias Lutz-Bachmann (Boston: MIT Press, 1997).

Brubaker, Rogers. *Citizenship and Nationhood in France and Germany* (Cambridge, Mass.: Harvard University Press, 1992).

———. *Nationalism Reframed: Nationhood and the National Question in the New Europe* (Cambridge University Press: Cambridge, 1997).

Brun-Rovet, Marianne. "A Perspective on the Multiculturalism Debate: *L'Affaire du Foulard* and *Laïcité* in France, 1989–1999," seminar paper, Harvard University, Department of Government. On file with the author.

Buchanan, Allen. "From Nuremberg to Kosovo: The Morality of Illegal International Legal Reform," *Ethics* 111 (July 2001): 673–705.

Butler, Judith. *Excitable Speech: Politics of the Performative* (New York and London: Routledge, 1997).

Cavallar, Georg. *The Rights of Strangers: Theories of International Hospitality, the Global Community and Political Justice since Vitoria* (Aldershot: Ashgate, 2002).

Cheah, Pheng, and Bruce Robbins (eds.). *Cosmopolitics: Thinking and Feeling Beyond the Nation* (Minneapolis: University of Minnesota Press, 1998).

Classen, Claus Dieter, ed. *Europa-Recht* (Munich: Deutscher Taschenbuch Verlag, 2005).

Commission de réflexion sur l'application du principe de laïcité dans la République. *Rapport au Président de la République* (Paris: Présidence de la République, 2003). Available at: http://www.ladocumentationfrancaise.fr/brp/notices/034000725.shtml.

Commissiong, Anand Bertrand. Review of David Held's *Global Covenant: The Social Democratic Alternative to the Washington Consensus,* in *Logos* 4, no. 2 (2005).

Connolly, William. *Pluralism* (Durham, N.C.: Duke University Press, 2005).

Conseil D'Etat, Assemblée générale (Section de l'intérieur). *Avis concernant le port à l'école de signes d'appartenance à une communauté religieuse.* no. 346.893–27, November 1989.

Convention on the Prevention and Punishment of the Crime of Genocide (Approved and proposed for signature and ratification or accession by General Assembly resolution 260 A (III) of December 9, 1948; entry into force January 12, 1951). United Nations, *Treaty Series,* vol. 78, 277–322.

Cover, Robert M. "*Nomos* and Narrative," *Harvard Law Review* 97, no. 1 (1983): 4–68.

Derrida, Jacques. "Signature, Event, Context" [1971], in *Limited Inc.* (Evanston, Ill.: Northwestern University Press, 1988).

———. "The Principle of Hospitality," *Parallax* 11, no. 1 (2005): 6–9.

———. *Adieu to Emmanuel Levinas* (Stanford: Stanford University Press, 1999).

———. *Of Hospitality. Anne Dufourmantelle invites Jacques Derrida to Respond,* trans. Rachel Bowlby (Stanford: Stanford University Press, 2000).

———. *On Cosmopolitanism and Forgiveness,* trans. Mark Dooley and Michael Hughes (London and New York: Routledge, 2001).

———. "Hostipitality" in *Acts of Religion,* ed. Gil Anidjar. (New York: Routledge, 2002).

———. *Rogues: Two Essays on Reason* (Stanford: Stanford University Press, 2005).

"Derrière la Voile." *Le Monde Diplomatique*, no. 599 (51) (February 2001): 6–10.

Doyle, Michael. "The New Interventionism," in *Global Justice*, ed. Thomas W. Pogge (Oxford: Basil Blackwell, 2001).

Dreyfus, Hubert L., and Paul Rabinow. *Michel Foucault: Beyond Structuralism and Hermeneutics* (Chicago: University of Chicago Press, 1982).

Felman, Shoshana. *The Juridical Unconscious: Trials and Traumas of the Twentieth Century* (Cambridge: Harvard University Press, 2002).

Ferrara, Alessandro. "On Boats and Principles: Reflections on Habermas's 'Constitutional Democracy,'" *Political Theory* 29, no. 6 (2001): 782–91.

Flikschuh, Katrin. *Kant and Modern Political Philosophy* (Cambridge: Cambridge University Press, 2000).

Foucault, Michel. *Power/Knowledge*, trans. and ed. Colin Gordon (New York: Pantheon Books, 1980).

———. *The Foucault Reader.* ed. Paul Rabinow (New York: Pantheon, 1984).

———. *Discipline and Punish: The Birth of the Prison*, trans. Alan Sheridan (New York: Pantheon Books, 1997).

Fraser, Nancy, "Foucault on Modern Power: Empirical Insights and Normative Confusions," *Praxis International* 1, no. 3 (October 1981): 272–287.

Free Ibrahim Web site: http://www.freeibrahim.com

Friedman, James. "Arendt in Jerusalem, Jackson at Nuremberg: Presuppositions of the Nazi War Crimes Trials," *Israel Law Review* 28, no. 4 (1994): 601–625.

Friedman, Thomas. *The Lexus and the Olive Tree* (New York: Farrar, Straus & Giroux, 1999).

Gaspard, Françoise, and Farhad Khosrokhavar. *Le Foulard et la République* (Paris: Découverte, 1995).

Giraud, Veronique and Yves Sintomer. *Alma et Lila Levy: Des Filles comme les Autres: Au-dela du Foulard.* Interviews by Veronique Giraud and Yves Sintomer (Paris: La Découverte, 2004).

Göle, Nilüfer. *The Forbidden Modern: Civilization and Veiling* (Ann Arbor: University of Michigan Press, 1996).

Habermas, Jürgen. *The Philosophical Discourse of Modernity: Twelve Lectures*, trans. Frederick Lawrence (Cambridge, Mass.: MIT Press, 1987).

———. "Kant's Idea of Perpetual Peace, with the Benefit of Two Hundred Years' Hindsight," in *Perpetual Peace: Essays on Kant's Cosmopolitan Ideal*, ed. James Bohman and Matthias Lutz-Bachmann (Boston: MIT Press, 1997).

———. *The Inclusion of the Other: Studies in Political Theory*, ed. Ciaran Cronin and Pablo De Greiff (Cambridge, Mass.: MIT Press, 1998).

———. *Between Facts and Norms*, trans. W. Regh (Cambridge, Mass.: MIT Press, 1996).

Hardt, Michael, and Antonio Negri. *Empire* (Cambridge, Mass.: Harvard University Press, 2000).

Hegel, G. W. F. *Hegel's Science of Logic*, 4th ed., trans. W. H. Johnston and L. G. Struthers (London: George Allen and Unwin; New York: Humanities Press, 1966).

———. *Phaenomenologie des Geistes* [1807], in *Hegels Werke*, Der philosophische Bibliothek, vol. 114 (Felix Meiner Verlag: 1956; 6th ed.); trans. A. V. Miller, and Analysis of the Text and Foreword by John Findlay, *Phenomenology of Spirit* (Oxford: Clarendon Press, 1977).

Held, David. *Democracy and the Global Order: From the Modern State to Cosmopolitan Governance* (Cambridge: Polity Press, 1995).

———. "Cosmopolitan Democracy and the Global Order: A New Agenda," in *Perpetual Peace: Essays on Kant's Cosmopolitan Ideal*, ed. James Bohman and Matthias Lutz-Bachmann (Boston: MIT Press, 1997).

———. "Law of States, Law of Peoples: Three Models of Sovereignty," *Legal Theory* 8 (2002): 1–44.

Hobbes, Thomas. *Leviathan*, ed. C. B. McPherson (London: Penguin Books [1651] 1968).

Hobsbawm, Eric. *Nations and Nationalism since 1780: Programme, Myth and Reality* (Cambridge: Cambridge University Press, 1990).

Hollifield, James F. *Immigrants, Markets, and States: The Political Economy of Postwar Europe* (Cambridge, Mass., and London: Harvard University Press, 1992).

Honig, Bonnie. "Declarations of Independence: Arendt and Derrida on the Problem of Founding a Republic," *American Political Science Review* 85, no. 1 (March 1991): 97–113.

———. *Political Theory and the Displacement of Politics* (Ithaca, NY: Cornell University Press, 1993).

Honig, Bonnie. "Dead Rights, Live Futures: A Reply to Habermas's 'Constitutional Democracy': The Paradoxical Union of Contradictory Principles?" *Political Theory* 29, no. 6 (2001): 792–805.

———. *Democracy and the Foreigner* (Princeton, N.J.: Princeton University Press, 2001).

———. "Bound by Law? Alien Rights, Administrative Discretion, and the Politics of Technicality: Lessons from Louis Post and the First Red Scare," in *The Limits of Law*, ed. Austin Sarat et al. (Stanford: Stanford University Press, 2005).

———. "The Time of Rights: Emergent Thoughts in an Emergency Setting," in, *The New Pluralism*, ed. Morton Schoolman and David Campbell (Duke University Press, forthcoming).

———. *Future Perfect* (unpublished manuscript).

Honneth, Axel. *The Critique of Power: Reflective Stages in a Critical Social Theory*, trans. Kenneth Baynes (Cambridge, Mass.: MIT Press, 1991).

Howard, Michael. "*Temperamenta Belli:* Can War be Controlled?" in *Restraints on War*, ed. Michael Howard (Oxford: Oxford University Press, 1979).

Ignatieff, Michael. *Human Rights as Politics and Idolatry*, with Commentary by K. Anthony Appiah, David Hollinger, Thomas W. Laquer, and Diane F. Orentlicher (Princeton, N.J.: Princeton University Press, 2001).

Jacobson, David. *Rights across Borders: Immigration and the Decline of Citizenship* (Baltimore and London: Johns Hopkins University Press, 1997).

Jaspers, Karl. *The Origin and Goal of History*, trans. Michael Bullock (New Haven, Conn.: Yale University Press, 1953).

Jay, Martin, and Leon Botstein. "Hannah Arendt: Opposing Views," *Partisan Review* 45, no. 3 (1978): 348–380.

Jay, Martin. *Permanent Exiles* (New York: Columbia University Press, 1986).

Kant, Immanuel. "Zum Ewigen Frieden. Ein philosophischer Entwurf" [1795], in *Immanuel Kants Werke (Shriften von 1790–1796)*, ed. A. Buchenau, E. Cassirer and B. Kellermann (Berlin: Verlag Bruno Cassirer, 1923).

———. "Die Metaphysik der Sitten in zwei Teilen" [1797], in *Immanuel Kants Werke (Shriften von 1790–1796)*, ed. A. Buchenau, E. Cassirer and B. Kellermann (Berlin: Verlag Bruno Cassirer, 1923).

———. *The Metaphysics of Morals*, trans. and ed. Mary Gregor (Cambridge: Cambridge University Press, 1996).

———. "Perpetual Peace: A Philosophical Sketch" [1795], in *Kant: Political Writings*, trans. H. B. Nisbet, ed. Hans Reiss, 2nd and enl. ed. (Cambridge: Cambridge University Press, 1994).

Kateb, George. *Hannah Arendt: Politics, Conscience, Evil* (Totowa, N.J.: Rowman and Allenheld, 1984).

———. "Political Action: Its Nature and Advantages," in *The Cambridge Companion to Hannah Arendt*, ed. Dana Villa, (Cambridge: Cambridge University Press, 2000).

Kelsen, Hans. *Pure Theory of Law*, trans. Max Knight (Berkeley and Los Angeles: University of California Press, [1934, 1960] 1967).

Kleingeld, Pauline. "Kant's Cosmopolitan Law: World Citizenship for a Global Order," *Kantian Review* 2 (1998): 72–90.

———. "Kant's Cosmopolitan Patriotism," *Kant-Studien*, Vol. 94 (2003): 299–316.

Koskenniemi, Martti. *The Gentle Civilizer of Nations: The Rise and Fall of International Law, 1870–1960* (Cambridge: Cambridge University Press, 2002).

Kotlowitz, Alex. "The Politics of Ibrahim Parlak: How did a political refugee who became a popular café owner in a small Michigan town suddenly become a terrorist in the eyes of the government? A post 9/11 story," *New York Times Magazine*, Mar. 20, 2005, p. 46.

Levinas, Emmanuel. *Totality and Infinity: An Essay on Exteriority*, trans. Alphonso Lingis (Pittsburgh, Pa.: Duquesne University Press, 1969).

Marshall, T. H. *Citizenship and Social Class and Other Essays* (Cambridge: Cambridge University Press, 1950).

Maus, Ingeborg. "Vom Nationalstaat zum Globalstaat oder: der Niedergang der Demokratie," in *Weltstaat oder Staatenwelt: Für und Wider die Idee einer Wletrepublik*, ed. Matthias Lutz-Bachmann and James Bohman (Frankfurt: Suhrkamp, 2002).

Metselaar, Suzanne. "When Neighbors Become Numbers: Levinas and the Inhospitality of Dutch Asylum Policy," *Parallax*, 11, no.1 (2005): 61–69.

Michelman, Frank. "Law's Republic," *Yale Law Journal* 97, no. 8 (July 1988): 1493–1537.

Mitscherlich, Alexander. *Society without the Father: A Contribution to Social Psychology*, trans. Eric Mosbacher (New York: Schocken Books [1963] 1970).

Misevic, Nenad. "Close Strangers: Nationalism, Proximity and Cosmopolitanism," *Studies in East European Thought* 51, no. 2 (1999): 109–125.

Multicultural Germany: Art, Performance, and Media. Special issue of *New German Critique*, 92 (Spring/Summer 2004).

Muthu, Sankar. *Enlightenment against Empire* (Princeton, N.J.: Princeton University Press, 2003).

Neuman, Gerald. "Human Rights and Constitutional Rights: Harmony and Dissonance," *Stanford Law Review* 55, no. 5 (May 2003): 1863–1901.

Nussbaum, Martha. "Patriotism and Cosmopolitanism," in *For Love of Country: Debating the Limits of Patriotism*, ed. Joshua Cohen (Boston, Mass.: Beacon Press, 1996).

O'Neill, Onora. *Bounds of Justice* (Cambridge: Cambridge University Press, 2000).

Power, Samantha. *A Problem from Hell: America and the Age of Genocide* (New York: Basic Books, 2003).

Rabkin, Jeremy A. *Law Without Nations: Why Constitutional Government Requires Sovereign States* (Princeton, N.J.: Princeton University Press, 2005).

Ratner, Steven R., and Jason S. Abrams. *Accountability for Human Rights Atrocities in International Law: Beyond the Nuremberg Legacy*, rev. and exp. ed. (New York: Clarendon Press: [1997] 2001).

Rawls, John. *A Theory of Justice* (Cambridge, Mass.: Harvard University Press, 1971).

———. *Political Liberalism* (New York: Columbia University Press, 1993).

———. *The Law of Peoples* (Cambridge, Mass.: Harvard University Press, 1999).

Renan, Ernest. "Qu'est-ce qu'une nation? (Paris: Calmann Lévy, 1882). English trans.: Renan, Ernest, "What is a Nation?" in *Nation and Narration*, ed. Homi K. Bhabha (New York: Routledge, 1990), pp. 8–22.

Rogin, Michael. *Ronald Reagan, the Movie, and Other Episodes in Political Demonology* (Berkeley: University of California Press, 1987).

Romig, Jeff. "Family, Friends Embrace Parlak," *South Bend Tribune*, June 4, 2005, p. A1. Available at http://www.harborcountry-news.com/articles/2006/03/23/news/story2.txt.

Rubenfeld, Jed. "The Two World Orders," *The Wilson Quarterly* 27, no. 4 (Autumn 2003): 22–36.

Sassen, Saskia. *Guests and Aliens* (New York: The New Press, 2000).

Schabas, William A. *An Introduction to the International Criminal Court* (Cambridge: Cambridge University Press, 2001).

Scheuerman, William E. *Liberal Democracy and the Social Acceleration of Time* (Baltimore and London: Johns Hopkins University Press, 2004).

Schmitt, Carl. *The Concept of the Political*, trans., intro., and notes by George Schwab (Chicago: University of Chicago Press, [1927] 1996).

——. *Das internationalrechtliche Verbrechen des Angriffskrieges und der Grundsatz, "Nullum crimen, nulla poena sine lege"* Published with annotations by Helmut Quaritsch (Berlin: Duncker and Humboldt, 1994).

Sciolino, Elaine. "French Islam Wins Officially Recognized Voice," *New York Times*, April 14, 2003, Sec. A, 4.

——. "Paris Journal; Back to Barricades: Liberty, Equality, Sisterhood," *New York Times*, August 1, 2003, sec. A, 4.

Simmel, Georg. "The Stranger" [1908], in *The Sociology of Georg Simmel*, trans. Kurt H. Wolff (Glencoe, Ill: Free Press, 1950).

Slaughter, Anne-Marie. "Leading Through Law," *The Wilson Quarterly* 27, no. 4 (Autumn 2003): 42–43.

Smith, Rogers M. "Beyond Tocqueville, Myrdal, and Hartz: The Multiple Traditions in America," *American Political Science Review* 87, no. 3 (1993): 549–566.

Soguk, Nevzat. *States and Strangers: Refugees and Displacements of Statecraft* (Minneapolis: University of Minnesota Press, 1990).

Stevens, Jacqueline. "Beyond Tocqueville, Please!" *American Political Science Review* 89, no. 4 (1995): 987–995.

Streinz, Rudolf, Christoph Ohler, and Christoph Herrmann, eds. *Die neue Verfassung fuer Europa* (Munich: C. H. Beck, 2005).

Teubner, Gunther, ed. *Global Law Without a State: Studies in Modern Law and Policy* (Aldershot and Brookfield, Vt.: Dartmouth Publishing Company, 1997).

Thomas, Monifa. "Jailed Immigrant to Get out on Bond," *Chicago Sun-Times*, May 21, 2005, p. 6.

Tuck, Richard. *The Rights of War and Peace: Political Thought and International Order from Grotius to Kant* (Cambridge: Cambridge University Press, 1999).

United Nations. *Charter of International Military Tribunal, in Agreement for the Prosecution and Punishment of the Major War Criminals of the European Axis*, 59 STAT. 1544, 82 UNTS 279, 1945.

———. *International Bill of Human Rights* (also *Universal Declaration of Human Rights*), UN Doc.A/Res/217(iii), 1948.

U.S. Representatives on the Commission of Responsibilities, *Memorandum of Reservations to the Majority Report*, April 4, 1919, excerpted in Michael Marrus, *The Nuremberg War Crimes Trial 1945–46: A Documentary History* (New York: Bedford/St. Martin's, 1997).

Waldron, Jeremy. "Minority Cultures and the Cosmopolitical Alternative," in *The Rights of Minority Cultures*, ed. Will Kymlicka (Oxford: Oxford University Press, 1995).

———. "What is Cosmopolitan?" *The Journal of Political Philosophy* 8, no. 2 (2000): 227–243.

Walzer, Michael. *Spheres of Justice: A Defense of Pluralism and Equality* (New York: Basic Books, 1983).

Walzer, Michael. "Liberalism and the Art of Separation," *Political Theory* 12, no. 3 (August 1984): 315–330.

Weber, Max. "Bureaucracy," in H. H. Gerth and C. Wright Mills (trans. and ed.), *From Max Weber: Essays in Sociology* (Oxford: Oxford University Press, 1958).

———. "The Types of Legitimate Domination," in *Economy and Society: An Outline of Interpretive Sociology*, ed. Guenther Roth and Claus Wittich (Berkeley: University of California Press, 1978).

Wischke, Mirko. "Die Politik der Menschenrechte im Zeitalter der Globalisierung: Zur aktuellen Diskussion in der Politischen Philosophie und Rechtsphilosophie," *Philosophische Rundschau* 49 (2002): 224–244.

Wittgenstein, Ludwig. *Philosophical Investigations*, the German text, with a revised English translation; trans. G. E. M. Anscombe (Malden, Mass.: Blackwell, 2001).

Zollberg, Aristide R., and Long Litt Woon. "Why Islam is like Spanish: Cultural Incorporation in Europe and the United States," *Politics and Society* 27, no. 1 (March 1999): 5–38.

Index

Power, Samantha, 180n15
private rights, 61
progressive time, 124n15
Protestantization of Islam, 58
public institutions, cosmopolitan
   norms and, 165

Rawls, John, 68
refugees, 46–47, 113, 162, 170, 171
remainders, of conditional
   hospitality, 113–114
revolutionary beginnings,
   paradoxes of, 72
rightful relations, in Kant's division of law, 21, 89, 148
right of asylum, 22, 25, 30
rights claims
   assessment of, 110
   and citizenship, 143n10
   natural right philosophies, 49
   private, 61
   undocumented aliens and, 46–47
   See also citizenship rights, dis-
      aggregation of; cosmopolitan
      rights; human rights
right to have rights, the, 106–108,
   117–118, 122n8
right-wing parties, in Europe, 61
Rome Treaty, 74
Rousseau, Jean-Jacques, 32, 87
rule of law, transformation of,
   176–177

sans papiers movement, 108–109
scarf affair. See l'affaire du foulard
   (the scarf affair)

Scheuerman, William E., 176
Schleswig-Holstein election laws,
   62–66
Schmitt, Carl, 38n5
self-constitution, and self-legislation, 33
separation, liberalism and, 59–60,
   71
Slaughter, Anne-Marie, 38–39n7
societies, interactions and independence of, 99n19
soft law, 42–43n26, 96
sovereignty
   devolution of, 170–171, 177
   Honig on Benhabib's treatment
      of, 114–115
   and hospitality, tension
      between, 31, 47
   liberal international, 23–24
   liberal model, 176
   popular, 33, 35, 63–64
   post-Westphalian models of,
      179n4
   power of, in rule of law,
      176–177
   territorial, vs. universal human
      rights, 30
   Westphalian, 23, 31
Stasi Commission Report, 76n17
state constitutions, monistic and
   dualistic, 181n18
statism, and paradox of democratic
   legitimacy, 115–116

temporalities, plural, 124n15
temporality, linear, 112

CPSIA information can be obtained at www.ICGtesting.com
Printed in the USA
BVOW011545141211

278343BV00001B/1/P